ACCESS TO ACADEMIC NETWORKS

Patrick J. Holligan

Published by
TAYLOR GRAHAM
on behalf of the
Primary Communications Research Centre
University of Leicester

Published on behalf of the Primary Communications Research Centre by

Taylor Graham
500 Chesham House
150 Regent Street
LONDON W1R 5FA

ISBN 0 947568 08 5

The opinions expressed in this report are those of the author and not necessarily those of the British Library

British Library Cataloguing in Publication Data

Holligan, Patrick J.
Access to academic networks.
1. Universities and colleges—Great Britain
—Data processing 2. Computer networks—
Great Britain
I. Title II. University of Leicester,
Primary Communications Research Centre
378.41'028546 LA637.7

ISBN 0-947568-08-5

CONTENTS

ABOUT PCRC

The Primary Communications Research Centre was established at the University of Leicester in 1976 with a grant from British Library (R&D) Department to act as a national focus for work in this field. The subject of primary communications covers all methods of disseminating research information, ranging from specialist journals and monographs to conferences and other informal methods. Staff at the Centre carry out research (both large and small-scale projects) into various factors affecting the dissemination, and all subject areas included - humanities, sciences, social sciences, medicine, agriculture and technology. Reports of this research are published as the projects are completed.

ABOUT THE AUTHOR

Patrick Holligan is a research associate with the Primary Communications Research Centre (PCRC), based at the University of Leicester. He has some eleven years' professional experience of the academic publishing industry, which includes six years spent with the Open University working on the preparation, production and marketing of multi-media course material.

His current research interests are concerned with establishing an experimental, network-based bulletin board for the Humanities, accessible initially from all universities and polytechnics in the UK. This work is funded by the British Library and is being undertaken under the auspices of the Office for Humanities Communication, also based at the University of Leicester.

Executive Summary

Computer networks are assuming an increasingly important role in the transmission and manipulation of information. A limited survey of six universities and two polytechnics was undertaken with the objective of examining the principal issues to emerge in the field of academic networking. The survey also considered the implications of current network developments in the context of new categories of services and users that are likely to emerge in parallel with existing network traffic which in character is represented almost exclusively by areas associated with data processing and computation.

Since the 1 April 1984 networking arrangements for the UK academic community have undergone significant changes. A process of extensive reorganisation is now evident at university computer centres, attributable, in the main, to the development of the Joint Academic Network (JANET) which will to a large extent replace the previous maze of inter-organisational leased-line and public network connections which was necessary to provide links between a variety of incompatible local computer operating environments. In conjunction with changes at a wide area (national) networking level a great deal of activity is also evident at local levels, concerning the up-grading of campus, or local area networks.

Full connectivity throughout the university community by means of JANET is now a functional reality, resulting for the first time in services such as electronic mail and computer conferencing being rendered practicable for a much wider constituency of users than was hitherto possible.

In practice, however, there are a number of issues that will have to be addressed before networks become established in the academic community as an acceptable medium for computer-mediated human communication. Until these can be resolved it may be some time before the full potential of electronic communications media is realised.

Factors affecting the growth of networking as a technique accessible to non-specialist academic staff and students in particular were as follows:

1. There is insufficient awareness of the potential of network applications; computer literacy and keyboard skills urgently require to be improved. More computer service support staff are needed to undertake educational and advisory roles in relation to new users - especially among subject fields outside the pure and applied sciences.

2. A national policy decision is required in relation to computer-mediated communication facilities such as electronic mail. At the present time local facilities in regard to this type of network application are insufficiently co-ordinated for the operation of a reliable mail service.

3. Closer monitoring of network services will be necessary to ensure their effective use - particularly in the context of new services such as electronic mail and conferencing.

4. The current provision of distributed terminals is insufficient. Improved terminal access is fundamental to the widespread adoption of network-based services such as on-line public access catalogues.

5. There is a need for more detailed research into the economics of network access. The present dearth of information is likely to result in inefficient practices being adopted. Means for the effective dissemination of such information are urgently required.

6. Centres of networking expertise have grown up around computer centres, libraries and other commercial information services. As campus networks are extended it will be necessary for these agencies to co-ordinate their efforts more closely, particularly if local facilities such as campus teletext, bulletin boards and on-line public access catalogues are to represent a functional utility for staff and students.

7. Network management will assume even greater importance in the future if more users and services are to be accommodated. Cutbacks in educational expenditure may result in network facilities being developed on a demand-driven basis. It is important that provision is made for those whose interest in networks lie in areas other than data processing, and that their needs are adequately represented in the allocation of funds and the assignment of priorities.

Introduction

> "For the academic community the convergence of computing and communication represents perhaps the most profound technical development since the invention of movable type and the modern printing press." (1)

This rather expansive assertion was made in 1981 by John W.McCredie, who at that time was president of EDUCOM, a US consortium of colleges and universities formed in 1964. The founding principle of the consortium was to establish a range of co-ordinated programmes the objective of which was to "actively co-operate to utilise information technology". As a result plans were made in 1966 for the establishment of an academic "network of networks" known as EDUNET, to be based on the concept of sharing computing resources to provide its member institutions with access to computer hardware and software at leading academic computer centres. Since that time the operation of the network has been extended to encompass many disciplines that lie outside areas usually associated with computing in the traditional sense of data processing or "number crunching", and services such as electronic mail have met with an enthusiastic response.

Consequently EDUCOM's considerable experience of computer-mediated communication lends weight to the above claim made by McCredie, which has served to inform this survey as an indication of the potential role of computer networks and their relevance for the academic community.

Relative to the US, distances and corresponding difficulties concerned with human communication are of a smaller scale in the UK. As a result perhaps, the origins of computer networks in Britain can be traced to the scientific community whose needs were based originally on the necessity for access to sophisticated, and therefore expensive, computing power. The ability to share resources by means of networked data communications obviated any unnecessary duplication of computing facilities and presented an attractive and cost-effective solution to the economic problems involved with providing sufficient access for researchers who were geographically dispersed among universities, polytechnics and national research laboratories.

Since the 1960s academic networks have, in the main, been developed along these lines. It is only comparatively recently that other computer-related applications, based on information rather than data processing, now offer a practicable means of supplementing, if not eventually superseding, existing methods of storing, retrieving and transmitting information. The written word, print on paper and oral communication, either by telephone or "face-to-face", are unlikely to be totally displaced by computer-mediated systems, but there are already indications to suggest that in certain instances facilities such as, for example, electronic mail and computer conferencing can offer distinct advantages over more established modes of human communication. If these techniques are sufficiently explored and developed within the acadmic community then McCredie's prognosis may indeed prove correct in relation to the future role of computer networks in the context of information management and the publishing process.

At the present time, however, the use of academic computer networks in the UK appears largely confined to the research scientist and computer specialist. If services of the nature outlined above are to gain common currency many problems will have to be tackled - not least of all those associated with developing greater levels of computer literacy among all categories of staff and students across traditional subject boundaries. A greater awareness of the range and complexion of network applications also requires to be promoted beyond those concerned with the pure and applied sciences.

In principle, the evolution of the Joint Academic Network (JANET) for universities, formally inagurated in April 1984, presents a unique opportunity for the realisation of services that were hitherto impracticable due to the fragmentation of existing facilities. In reality a number of fundamental issues remain to be addressed at both policy and practical levels before the academic community will benefit from what is, for the first time, a unified and fully integrated private computer network.

This survey seeks to identify the main considerations to emerge from an examination of a limited sample of institutions which, in common with all UK universities, are in the process of up-grading local campus networks and network-based services, thereby providing improved access both to the national academic network and other academic and commercial networks available via the public telecommunications utilities.

Methodology

This report represents the results of a six-month investigation undertaken during the period January to June 1985, concerning network access at universities in the UK and, in particular, the potential of networks for computer-mediated communication, as opposed to their established role in areas associated with data processing and computation.

Preliminary investigations demonstrated that existing network provision at universities is currently in the process of significant reorganisation. Prior to embarking on any form of survey it was considered desirable to obtain a wider perspective of the nature and rationale for these changes. A series of ten interviews were subsequently conducted involving what may be loosely defined as an "expert panel", comprising senior representatives operating at policy level in a number of organisations concerned either directly with networks in a computing context, or indirectly in terms of being responsible for the development of network-based services. This panel encompassed areas which include university computing in a national context, library co-operatives and other commercial library services, academic publishers, the book trade, the Booksellers and Publishers Associations, and research interests relevant to the development of computer-based, networked communications.

The conclusion of this aspect of the enquiry indicated that a comprehensive survey by postal questionnaire was clearly inappropriate as such a course was unlikely to prove informative given the timing of the survey and the complex nature of the issues involved. The apparent state of flux current at many universities concerning work on implementing local services associated with Joint Academic Network (JANET) and upgrading and extending local campus networks also influenced the formulation of an alternative approach.

In the face of such shifting ground it was decided instead to present a "snapshot" of networking activity at a number of selected sites, together with an examination of the principal issues to emerge from this exercise. Six universities were examined on the basis of their existing use of networks and in relation to set of criteria set out below: (i) large civic; (ii) small civic; (iii) campus structure; (iv) collegiate structure; (v) science/technology orientation; (vi) humanities orientation.

By taking this approach it was hoped to obtain a reasonably representative picture of current networking practices. It also formed a basis for examining the conditions under which computer-mediated "human" networks might prove a practicable alternative (or addition) to more traditional methods of communication.

Polytechnics do not come within the terms of reference of this report, but it was considered useful to include two such institutions as their present position is quite different from that of the universities with regard to network access. The main part of the survey comprised a programme o. structured interviews involving what may be termed a "practitioner panel". Two principal areas were isolated as representing the focus for the majority of current university networking activity; namely, the computing centre or laboratory and the library. Where possible research groups were also consulted if they could be identified as using or planning to use computer networks for communications rather than data handling purposes.

The author is grateful to the members of both panels who were most generous with their time. In many instances interviews sparked further discussions due to the degree of interest that the subject is capable of generating - particularly among those more closely involved with network planning and its consequent implications for university research, teaching and administration in the future. In most instances individuals and institutions have not been directly identified in this report, as this was the basis on which the survey was conducted: consequently the observations of most panel members consulted were advanced in perhaps more forthright terms than might have been the case had the survey been conducted at a distance and by less direct means.

1 What is a computer network?

Stated simply a computer network can be explained in terms of three principal elements which comprise the basis for current developments observed in this survey of the university computing community, namely:

The Physical Network;
The Conceptual Network;
The Human Network.

The Physical Network

The three elements of a computer network listed above can be thought of as layers that lie one upon the other representing an order of increasing technical complexity. The physical layer, often referred to as the sub-network, is a fundamental requirement for any networking configuration as it provides the communications path or signal carrier enabling computers and peripheral equipment such as terminals, printers and storage devices to be interconnected over distances ranging from a matter of metres to many thousands of kilometres.

The Conceptual Network

The next layer in the network model refers to the potential for linking a number of computers, by means of the physical network, in a manner that enables data to be exchanged in an intelligible common format through the use of a set of standard rules or "protocols". These protocols allow computers to communicate with each other at any point on the conceptual network which supports a facility for what is known as "interworking". Computers connected in this fashion may be said to constitute a conceptual network.

The Human Network

A conceptual network based on interworking relates essentially to establishing communications between computers for the purpose of accessing complex processing power not available at a local site. A human network, by contrast, concerns computer users themselves who wish to establish personal contact with each other for the purposes of human communication rather than data transmission. This aspect of networking has been described as "an extension of the very nature of computers, offering the same precise, effective means of transporting information that computers offer in the processing of information". (2)

1.1 THE ACADEMIC NETWORKING COMMUNITY - BACKGROUND

Networks were originally developed as a means of providing researchers, initially the high energy physics community, with access to computing facilities based on hardware that by today's standards was extremely expensive. In 1964 the computing needs for all UK universities were provided by a single Ferranti Atlas machine based at the Rutherford Appleton Laboratory at a cost of £27m at current prices. Today an ICL PERQ computer offers the same amount of processing power at a fraction of the cost (1/2000th) and physical size of the early Atlas installation which occupied an entire building.

Hardware costs fell dramatically over the next twenty years enabling universities to provide their own local computing facilities, but the cost of developing sophisticated applications software remained extremely high and it was in this context that the concept of "resource sharing" was evolved, based originally on a private network operating between the national research laboratories at Daresbury and Rutherford which was later expanded to become SERCNet (the Science and Engineering Research Council Network). In 1982 the SERCNet was available from most universities throughout the country by a variety of network routes and in 1983 provided facilities for some 3000 grant-holders. The role of SERCNet was to provide access to computing resources for specific projects involving the universities and where financial resources were unavailable through either the UGC or Computer Board. In 1983 it was estimated that the SERC's total computing provision averaged about £16m annually of which £5m was capital and £11m recurrent expenditure.

There are three routes by which universities obtain funding for computing facilities; the SERC, mentioned above, the UGC general funding provision (of which it has been estimated the universities spend a total in excess of £50m on computing) and the Computer Board.

The Computer Board was established in 1966 to act for the Department of Education Science (DES) in co-ordinating and supporting provision of computing facilities for universities. Its annual budget is in the region of £29m (£12m on capital and £17m on recurrent expenditure). The organisation of university computing is operated on a two-tier structure in which each university has its own local facility backed up by the major national centres at London and Manchester which provided software support and access to more powerful computer installations. From the outset a high priority has been placed on providing access to data communications for the computing community. What were known in topological terms as "star networks" formed around the national centres, being further augmented in the 1970s by the appearance of extensive regional star networks, including:

GANNET (North-West Universities Network)
Keele, Liverpool, Lancaster, Salford, Manchester, UMIST.

SWUCN (South-West Universities Computer Network)
Bath, Bristol, Exeter, University of Wales Institute of Science and Technology, University College Cardiff, University of Wales College of Medicine.

MIDNET (Midlands Universities Network)
Nottingham, Leicester, Loughborough, Aston,

Birmingham, Warwick. (This regional network was planned in the late 70s following publication of the Wells Report and just before plans were laid for a national network - see below.)

As data communications activity increased an urgent need arose to rationalise the national university networking structure to permit not only resource sharing between members of regional networks, but a fully integrated computing environment based on the concept of interworking between several types of different proprietory hardware configurations and software operating systems. The first step in this direction was taken by the Computer Board in 1973 with the establishment of a working party whose brief was to make recommendations regarding the future direction of networking. There followed in 1976 the publication of the Wells Report which recommended that:

(a) collaboration between the Computer Board and the Research Councils be strengthened with a view to effecting economies in the provision of communications networks and network-related facilities;

(b) the Computer Board allocate at least three per cent of its annual hardware expenditure to the provision of network facilities;

(c) the Board and Research Councils set up a small full-time unit to co-ordinate, guide and rationalise network development involving those bodies receiving their principal funding from the DES.

These requirements coincided with a number of projects being developed to standardise the various different types of network links that had evolved within the regions and between the major national computer centres. In 1979 the Joint Network Team (JNT) [unless otherwise stated the term "JNT" is used throughout as a convenient shorthand to denote both the Joint Network Team and Network Executive] was set up to develop a cost-saving approach to this problem which led to the commissioning of 40 development projects aimed at eventually creating an "open working" computing environment based on a set of standard protocols which would enable networking between different manufacturers' computer equipment.

Linking university sites across the country involves what is known as "wide area networks" (WANs). At a local level the rapid fall in the cost of computer hardware allowed universities to purchase small, yet powerful minicomputers and situate them in department buildings either on a campus or across distributed sites. Linking these computers involves the principle of "local area networks" (LANs) which presented a further problem to the network planners as some means had to be developed for connecting LANs to WANs for a fully integrated national network to be feasible. Since the proposal for a single, unified private academic network became the responsibility of the Network Management Committee in 1981 a great deal of work has been necessary in the adoption and implementation of non-proprietor standards aimed at achieving a fully integrated physical network.

1.2 THE JOINT ACADEMIC NETWORK (JANET)

The Joint Academic Network, or JANET as it is known, was formally inaugurated on the 1 April 1984. At the time of writing physical connections have been installed at all universities in the UK "with the specific intention of evolving from the present rather _ad hoc_ provision to a single network, using common standards, and to which ny member of the academic community will have access". (3) This process of evolution is based on the establishment of an integrated conceptual network through the application of standard protocols.

(a) Wide Area Networks (WANs) and Common Standards

Work on adopting a set of common standards for the Joint Academic Network predated what is now commonly referred to as the Open Systems Interconnection (OSI) model based on the recommendations of bodies including ISO (International Standards Organisation), ECMA (European Computer Manufacturers Organisation) and the CCITT (International Telegraph and Telephone Consultative Committee). Agreement on the complete set of protocol definitions for the OSI model are not likely to emerge for several years, consequently the Joint Network Team has produced interim protocols called Rainbow Books - each network service being denoted by a colour code, e.g. electronic mail is known as "Grey Book". Althugh the basis of the Rainbow Books is similar to the OSI model, complete transition to the new ISO standards is certain to take some considerable time and effort.

The basis on which JANET operates is CCITT recommendation X.25 for packet-switched wide area networks. Development of these standards has been carried out by a variety of interest groups sponsored by the Department of Trade and Industry, British Telecom and the JNT; as a result JANET, although a private network, is compatible with BT's own PSS (Packet Switch Stream) public data network.

(b) Packet Switching

Packet switching in relation to networking technology offers significant economic benefits for data transmission through better performance, more efficient use of line connections and greatly improved reliability. Developed originally in the early 1960s by Donald Davies of the UK National Physical Laboratory and Larry Roberts of the US Department of Defense Advanced Research Projects Agency (ARPA), packet switching now forms the basis of wide area networking in many countries, and was introduced in the UK as a fully operational service in 1981.

In simple terms packet switching relates to the nature in which data signals are transmitted by computers, commonly described as "bursty", because the intervals between segments of transmitted data are relatively long. This meant in effect that prior to the introduction of packet switching establishing a network connection between computers involved maintaining thc link throughout the entire duration of a transaction despite that in aggregrate terms the actual time required for the exchange of data might only represent a fraction of the total connection time. By contrast, packet switching, as the name suggests, breaks signals up into packets or blocks of data which are allocated bandwidth only when they have been filled and are ready for transmission. In this way data from several sources can be interleaved and sent to different destinations on the network to be reassembled on arrival by means of a routeing address tagged to each packet. Error checking routines ensure that if signals are incorrectly received an automatic request for retransmission is initiated. Interest in this form of network communication was stimulated by the information processing industry whose rapid growth had made reliable, error-free data transmission essential.

The South-West Universities Computer Network (SWUCN) was the first region to introduce X.25 packet switching in 1982, thereby allowing any terminal connected to the network from members' sites access to SWUCN's ICL 2980 mainframe (and any other computer on the network as since 1976 all SWUCN's new mainframe computers had to be capable of operating regional communication standards prior to the introduction of the X.25 protocol). Featured in Computer Weekly in November 1983 SWUCN stated:

> "X.25 standardisation has allowed us to plan confidently knowing that no matter what requirements emerged we would be able readily to adapt the shape of our network. X.25 wide area communication is now running in parallel with development work on LANs and in step with the plans for JANET, linking all the UK universities. The target is to allow the computer terminal on a researcher's desk access to all data processing facilities and to other external services via PSS."(4)

Network facilities of the type outlined above are now available to the whole academic community via JANET and their implementation will, in the view of the JNT, devolve to each university and its computer centre. The rate at which the full set of Rainbow Book services are adopted will depend on local priorities, financial resources and demand.

(c) Value-added Services on JANET

As a physical network JANET simply offers a means of moving data from one computer to another. At the level of the conceptual network a number of value-added applications are provided to enhance its utility. These include protocols for connecting different types of terminal to the network, transferring files, and jobs to remote host computers, and providing an electronic mail handling facility. Under the Rainbow Book scheme they can be summarised as follows:

Table 1.1 Network Services on JANET

Function	Rainbow Book
Network service	Yellow
Terminal access	Green
File transfer	Blue
Job transfer	Red
Electronic mail	Grey
Network access (to PSS and other X.25 networks)	Orange
Network access (via "CR82" protocol for Cambridge ring LANs)	- (CCITT recommendation)

Regional computer networks will eventually be dismantled as their function has now been largely superseded by JANET. Major university computer centres will, however, fufil an important role in the national network structure, operating as JANET Packet Switching Exchanges (JPSEs) and Network Operation Centres (NOCs) in conjunction with the national research councils' computing laboratories. Access to the network is provided at a minimum of 9.6 kbits/s with some sites connected at 48 kbits/s. The main problem identified with WANs is their relatively low speed of operation when compared with evolving LAN technologies like Cambridge rings and ethernets, which are capable of operating at speeds in the order of megabits per second. Recent experimental work on high-performance packet switching techniques like the Universe project have been investigating the prospects of using satellite links to overcome such difficulties in relation to wide area networking.

(d) Local Area Networks (LANS)

In the strictest sense of the definition a LAN is normally considered to operate over a limited distance within a building at a theoretical speed of up to 100 M.bits/s. In the context of academic networks, however, a LAN is generally synonymous with what is referred to as the "campus network", of which there are three principal types in current operation, namely: X.25-based CPSEs (Campus Packet Switching Exchanges), Cambridge rings and, more recently, ethernets. The most widespread LAN system in use is the X.25 CPSE, largely due to the maturity of the technology, but some universities have been experimenting with high-performance campus networks based on Cambridge ring and ethernet technologies operating at effective speeds of between 10 to 60 M.bits/s. Several universities now possess combined CPSE/ring or CPSE/ethernet campus networks and a considerable amount of work has been done on interfacing between systems in order to provide users with a "gateway" to the WAN and other networks services available only via PSS. At the end of 1982 there were 27 universities using X.25 CPSEs and eight with Cambridge rings (there was no recorded use of ethernets at that time). On the basis of a limited sample of institutions visited for the purposes of this report it was evident that several were in the process of introducing ethernets in preference to Cambridge rings since this LAN technology appears to becoming the adopted standard outside the UK - particularly in the US.

In networking terms LANs have enabled improved distributed terminal access across campuses and between remote sites, allowing users to link into a variety of local computing facilities (including the potential for campus mail systems) and JANET. Network connections will be possible from offices, departments, colleges, halls of residence and libraries.

Provided local computer centres have implemented the "Grey Book" protocol it is also possible, in principle, to use electronic mail between any university in the UK, and access to other national and international academic and commercial networks is now technically more straightforward. In practice, however, these facilities are subject to a number of qualifications which will be examined.

1.3 SUMMARY

The rationalisation of network provision for the universities into one interconnected community, represented by JANET, provides a practical model on which to outline the essential functions of a physical and conceptual network. The adoption of common standards for wide area networking and the extension of value-added services at a local level through the implementation of Rainbow Book protocols have provided the basic conditions necessary for national and international human networks to evolve on a more accessible scale than has previously existed. Local campus networks, as they are expanded, will permit the connection of a significantly enlarged and distributed terminal population - as noted in 1983 by a Computer Board working party on computer facilities for teaching in universities:

> "Computer communications can be used for electronic mail and telesoftware. Such communications are wider than purely lecturer-lecturer and can extend to student-lecturer and student-student links.
> It is now possible for lecturers to transmit information to students in this way and for students to prepare their work on a computer, send it to a lecturer for marking by simple file transfer and for the lecturer to return the marked work in the same way. These communications have an obvious role to play where the student body is physically dispersed."(5)

That this does not appear to be happening to any significant extent indicates the existence of a number of problems associated with network access and are relevant in a wider context as they relate to the conditions under which human computer-mediated communication is feasible.

The emphasis placed on JANET up to this point reflects the importance of its role in the academic community, as it is almost certainly the vehicle upon which a major proportion of network traffic will be carried for the foreseeable future. The expansion of human communication via computer networks is therefore ultimately linked to the development of JANET as a means of providing relatively cheap and reliable routes to other networks and network-based services.

2 What is computer-mediated communication?

As indicated in Section 1, it is at the human layer of the network model that the most complex technical problems are encountered. Resource sharing for the purposes of data processing consists typically of moving between two computing environments in order, for example, to enable a local computer to access another more powerful or specialised remote facility. This was the basis on which SERCNet and what has been described as "the maze of ad hoc connections between universities" were originally developed. For human, computer-mediated communication to represent a practicable utility there must first exist a viable population of users who are able to exchange information by means of moving freely between a variety of computing configurations and operating systems.

Difficulties associated with "interworking" in the context of the physical and conceptual network have to a large extent been overcome through the introduction of JANET and the interim protocols. As more universities implement Grey Book mail the potential for human networking will assume greater visibility and demand can be expected to increase as users begin to have access to desk-top workstations, enabling services such as mail and computer conferencing to play a more routine part in their work patterns.

The introduction of the ARPANET in the US in the late 1960s intended from the outset to provide a number of messaging facilities as a means of linking project directors and program managers. By 1973 the convenience of electronic mail had been widely recognised by many other users of the network and its rapid adoption came as a surprise to planners. A similar situation may eventually occur on the UK academic network as access becomes more widespread.

> "Until recently electronic mail and conferencing have not been given a high priority by comparison with other computing-related applications. This situation has changed to some extent and electronic mail is now recognised as a legitimate and important element of the JANET network."(6)

A trend towards the rapid adoption of electronic mail and conferencing
services by the academic community can be observed in the US where human networks were being planned by the Inter-University Communications Council as early as 1964 through the foundation of EDUCOM. Following a symposium in 1966 EDUCOM proposed the creation of EDUNET, a computer-based inter-institutional network whose objectives were not simply to promote the concept of resource sharing within the computing community, but to extend the medium to "link scholars together no matter where they were located". At the end of 1984 EDUNET's membership included 143 colleges and universities with gateways to a further 300 institutions.

> "Telemail and conferencing continued to dominate the network, accounting for approximately two-thirds of all resource traffic. Communications among various discipline oriented subgroups within and among institutions was the main use of these systems."(7)

In the context of this US example of a human network it has been suggested that it reflects several underlying features of American higher education. Scholars tended to identify with their own disciplines rather than with a department, college, or university. Often only a small group of individuals shared common research interests within a single department and their natural affinity with other researchers, no matter how widely dispersed led to efforts to establish computer-based networks for the purposes of human communication.

> "We want a network because it will provide ... research tools for the community at reasonable cost and in reasonable time. The network will be a service facility for all ... regardless of their field, location, or their

resources. It will provide a communications system that will help those in this emerging field [cognition] to talk to each other despite the fact that they are in different departments and at different universities. ... Most important it will provide these capabilities in a way that will grow with the field and be shaped by the field in a manner of its own devising."(8)

The concept of shaping the network medium has proved particularly important in the design of computer-mediated communications systems such as conferencing and mail, as users are likely to be antagonistic towards a technology that requires them to adapt existing work patterns in a manner that is cumbersome or unnatural.

2.1 COMPUTER CONFERENCING AND MAIL

It has been predicted that by the 1990s computer conferencing will be as widely used as the telephone is today. It may, in addition, affect the degree of decentralisation available to organisations by substituting communication for travel, and provide new opportunities for the formation of special interest groups and "invisible colleges".

The first computerised conferencing system was developed in the US in 1970, known as the Electronic Information Exchange Systems for Scientific Research Communities. EIES was designed to replicate existing forms of communication in the scientific community. (See Table 2.1)

(a) Messaging: a facility to send short informal messages to an individual, a number of specific individuals or a whole group.

(b) Conferencing: a topic-orientated discussion in which a permanent transcript of the proceedings is built up.

(c) Notebooks: refers to a user's private on-line space for composing, storing and reorganising items of work with the aid of computer-assisted techniques for manipulating and editing entries. These items could on completion (or in draft) be sent to colleagues as mail for comments or entered publicly in the conference section for similar purposes.

(d) Bulletin Boards: usually a public on-line facility for entering news, information and announcements. They can also be used for open letters and short discussion papers.

Table 2.1 EIES Communication Features (9)

Structure and Function	Replaces
Messages	Letters Telephone Face-to-face conversations Visits
Conferences	Face-to-face conferences or meetings
Notebooks	Sending drafts or preprints Necessity for co-authors to be co-located
Bulletin Boards	Newsletters (eventually journals and abstract services)

Throughout the 1970s a number of US experimental conferencing and mail systems were developed including:

EMISARI - System Evaluation Division of the Executive Office of the President;

FORUM - a development on the EMISARI model used by the US Institute for the Future;

PLANET - a simplified version of FORUM;

CONFER - developed by the University of Michigan;

ORACLE - developed by Northwestern University;

CONCLAVE - message and conferencing system developed first in UK then by General Conferencing Systems Ltd. (US);

HERMES - Bolt, Beranek and Newman - originally contractors for the ARPANET;

MAILBOX - Scientific Timesharing Inc.

By 1977 it was estimated that about 300 researchers were engaged in experimenting with these systems, including a large proportion of Swedish users who had a strong interest in the development of computer conferencing. The Swedish National Defence Institute was at that time split over three different locations and it was estimated that face-to-face conferences were costing $28 per hour compared with $10 per hour for a computer conferencing facility. Aside from the economic advantages it was also observed that for a large part of the year Sweden is subject to severe weather making extensive travel less attractive by comparison with the obvious advantages of computer-based communication. The Swedish programme resulted in the formation of "COM", based on the earlier US EIES and PLANET-FORUM systems.

Located at the University of Stockholm COM has extended its national membership, put at upwards of 1400, to most western European countries and the US. In 1984 COM handled more than 180,000 written entries per year and provided reading access to more than three million conference entries. A UK version of COM is now hosted by the University of York with a gateway facility to COM at Stockholm. For those academic users who have access to York via JANET, COM has in many instances provided the first opportunity of experimenting with the computer conferencing medium.

2.2 EFFECTS ON EXISTING COMMUNICATIONS MEDIA

It is difficult to advance any precise judgement on the actual current effects of computer-mediated communications over existing media such as the telephone and postal services. Within the UK academic community network traffic statistics for JANET have only recently begun to be compiled and do not separate mail from general data traffic. The same situation obtained at local sites where, to date, mail represents an insignificant element of campus network traffic, which at the present time does not justify the overheads of traffic monitoring. The JNT see their task as principally that of providing a stable and reliable national network service for the universities, "but what people do [on JANET] is largely up to themselves - the same applies for conferencing". In the opinion of the JNT "It would be a mistake to assume that networking will lead to any marked fall in the use of the telephone and postal services; networks may instead provide additional resources to complement existing modes of communication". (6)

There is, however, some evidence to show that where practicable messaging systems are available the rate of adoption appears to be quite dramatic. (See Tables 2.2-2.4.)

Results of a survey undertaken by COM at Stockholm demonstrate that while effects can be detected on telephone usage, face-to-face conferences and to a lesser extent the postal service and internal mail, memos etc. the most marked effect appeared to be in generating completely new communication networks. (This was a limited survey of 112 COM users at the Swedish National Defense Research Institute chosen from those who had experience of more than 100 COM conferencing sessions and who had also used the system in the two months immediately preceding the investigation - see Table 2.5.)

Table 2.2 Prestel (10)

Number of mailbox messages	Number of information frames accessed	Year
315,000	84.1 m	1982
715,000	152 m	1983
3,996,000	220 m	1984
5,980,000	390 m	1985

Table 2.3 COM Computer Conferencing Usage (11)

Total hours	Year
9,000	1979
15,000	1980
24,000	1981
26,000	1982
35,000	1983

Table 2.4 MAILNET (US academic network) (12)

Period Sept-Sept 1983-84	Mail Messages	Cumulative Users
1st Quarter	2,200	500
2nd "	6,200	2,500
3rd "	11,000	7,000
4th "	15,000	9,100

Table 2.5 Which Media has COM Replaced? (13)

Replaces	% messages written on COM	% messages read on COM	% time spent on COM
Letters, handwritten notes, circulars etc.	7	4	6
Telephone calls	23	8	14
Different kinds of face-to-face meetings	17	11	13
New communication which would not have occurred without COM	50	75	65
Other media (not specified)	3	2	2

One of the main conclusions drawn by the COM survey was that while users initially regarded computer mail and conferencing as a substitute for existing media attitudes changed as they became familiar with the technology. In time conferencing was instead considered to offer new possibilities for wider communication with people whom users would otherwise not have had occasion to contact and substituted for traditional media only in circumstances where a clear advantage was demonstrated.

These findings are also reinforced by an EIES study (14) which found that conference and mail systems would only be adopted if the perceived rewards were greater than the operational overheads, represented in terms of time, ease of use and economic factors. In looking at barriers to use a number of interesting points were noted that still require to be resolved in the context of evolving human networks in the UK academic community.

2.3 BARRIERS TO HUMAN NETWORKING

The purpose of a computer-mediated human network, as observed earlier, is to link people rather than machines, which requires that the original concept of resource sharing be extended along the lines proposed by the JNT for open working through the adoption of the Open Systems Interconnection model.

Many of the existing barriers to network access for computing applications also relate to those principles necessary for establishing practicable human communications networks.

1. Access to terminals: for services such as mail and conferencing to be used effectively "mailboxes", whether located on a local or remote computer host require to be consulted regularly. The COM survey found that the introduction of these services was significantly inhibited if people had to move between buildings or even between offices to gain access to a terminal. Current work on extending campus networks, thereby increasing the distributed terminal population, will be an important factor in determining the rate at which local access is improved. This will in turn depend on the level of funding available and the nature of local priorities for computing services. As one computer centre stated in relation to the Computer Board's 1983 working party report:

   > "Since the early nineteen seventies technology has made the provision of computer facilities on a wide scale much more feasible, particularly since the advent of powerful, cheap microcomputers, and this is reflected in the extent of facilities recommended in the Report ... However the financial climate in higher education has worsened greatly in the past decade and evidence of this is the lack of any new money being made available by the DES to support the Report's widely acclaimed recommendations." (15)

2. Education: there appears a pressing need to provide adequate training for first-time users and those who

do not regularly make use of computing facilities. A recent survey which looked at computer provision in the humanities pinpointed this area of difficulty - as one university computing services section stated: "We are only now trying to get to grips with providing more tuition to the neglected part of our community - mainly the arts people". (16) User manuals, typically in excess of 100 pages, were not felt to be useful for the "naive user". Short courses, personal tuition and on-line training sessions will be necessary if significant advances are to be made in this area.

3. Critical mass: for electronic mail to offer a practicable service there must first exist a viable, interconnected network population. Mail systems are heavily used between computer centres because in addition to being conversant with the technology users generally have their own desk-top terminals and therefore the likelihood of being able to reach colleagues is very high. They are also linked by common interests.

The same principle applies to small subject-orientated groups or "invisible colleges". It was observed by the EIES survey that if such a network was not carefully planned participants would be unlikely to devote time to using a conferencing system to contact people with whom they had little in common. The minimum number of active participants was found to be in the order of eight to twelve spread over three or more geographical locations. Below this number it was unlikely that the network would generate a sufficient number of new items to maintain interest. A larger group membership promoted a higher degree of interest and motivated users to participate with greater frequency.

4. Ease of use: the COM study demonstrated that many first-time users related new types of activity to existing work systems with which they were familiar. (This concept has now been adopted by a new generation of microcomputers that use "icons" to represent functions such as filing, word processing the creation of personal databases and mail as a series of pictograms such as a filing tray, a pen, or an index card.) Networks also require to be made more "user friendly" by offering

assistance through the use of menu-driven rather than command-driven operator prompts.

A more serious problem exists in the context of electronic mail. Users' "mailboxes" can either be located centrally, as in the case of COM at York, or locally, spread over a number of "mailserver" computers - ideally one at each site of a distributed campus. The need for a national register of networked computers has been apparent for some time but is now particularly urgent as more network hosts become available on JANET. The result has been the Name Registration Scheme (NRS) whose objectives are:

(a) to provide a unique name for each host which can be used uniformly throughout the academic community (and by those coming into JANET from other networks) for identification purposes;

(b) to provide associated addressing and other information for use by users and local network managers in setting up network access tables (or directories).

Work on developing the NRS has been undertaken for the JNT by Salford University and it is hoped that all universities will register their local services (and update information as necessary), to enable wide area network connections to be made simply and in a standard, unambiguous format. For example:

TONY SMITH @ UK. AC. SALFORD. R-D

TONY SMITH: mail recipient's registered name
UK: for incoming international traffic
AC: routeing to the academic network (JANET)
SALFORD: address of institution contacted
R-D: registered name of campus mailserver on which Tony Smith's mail is located

One also needs to know the registered name used by the mail recipient : is it A. Smith, Tony Smith, Antony Smith, Anthony Smith, Dr. Prof. etc? It will be necessary for local on-line directories to be provided with this type of information and, in addition, an ability to assist users by means of "fuzzy sets" (searching mechanisms that can offer a selection of possibilities in the event of receiving an ambiguous, misspelt or incorrect name). Much work still requires to be done in this area.

5. Adaptability: network planning must make provision for expansion, by being able to accommodate larger terminal populations and new services such as on-line public access catalogues (OPACS) and campus teletext systems. Increased traffic can cause response rates to drop to unacceptable levels and therefore network management will play an increasingly important role in the future. (For example, Strathclyde University has recently announced its intention to provide each of its 7000 students with a portable workstation and the capability of "continuous access to the [campus] network".(17)

2.5 SUMMARY

Having outlined the functions of the physical and conceptual layers of a network the intention has been to indicate the nature of human networks and the types of services likely to emerge. There is evidence to show that where new services demonstrate perceived they tend to be adopted with enthusiasm. In the US the scale of physical distances offer obvious potential for mail in terms of speed, cost and efficiency. In Sweden climatic conditions uncondusive to extensive travel have also been advanced as reasons for the interest shown in computer conferencing.

The potential for forming "invisible colleges" and the relative ease with which they can be joined are also factors that commend computer-mediated communication to the academic community. In this context it has been claimed that the tradition of free and open interchange of information between academics makes networking an obvious channel for communication, particularly as the sheer volume of research has led to a bottleneck in conventional means of publishing topical research, creating a backlog of working papers, drafts, pre-prints etc.

At the present time, however, it is generally held that new forms of computer-based communication have not as yet had any marked effect upon traditional media, but have instead been used to complement their use where applications are judged appropriate. Exactly what is considered appropriate in the UK context turns largely upon what is currently feasible in terms of finance, planning and network development rather than the technology itself. Local access is also a major consideration for the academic community as the results of the following survey demonstrate.

3 Access to networks

All computer centres visited for the purposes of their survey reported that prior to April 1984 it had been necessary to use a variety of networks to achieve an adequate measure of connectivity for the provision of data communications associated with their computing services. The most commonly used networks were the SERCNet, PSS, regional computer networks and a maze of ad hoc connections to national computer centres. Dial-up acess via PSTN was also used, but principally by libraries and from remote areas of university sites that had to use this route as a means of accessing the local network.

With the exception of the polytechnics network access now comprises two main routes, namely JANET and the public networks represented by PSS, and, in the case of libraries, PSTN. The rationalisation of networking arrangements for the academic community since April 1984 now offers full connectivity between 150 university and research council sites. Because JANET's networking facilities are effectively free to users this route has been adopted for academic traffic wherever possible. Although all universities visited were physically connected to the network there was some variation in the rate at which the complete set of Rainbow Book protocols was being adopted. In many instances job transfer (Red Book) and electronic mail (Grey Book) were awaiting implementation.

The immediate consequence of JANET has been a marked drop in PSS usage to the extent that one university computing centre met all traffic charges (excluding the library, which used PSTN dial-up connections as it did not have access to PSS). This was an atypical occurence, based on a remarkably low incidence of local demand. At every other institution access to PSS was by arrangement and on a strictly "pay as you use" basis.

Aside from the private academic network and PSS, two institutions reported using an informal network called USENET which can be accessed in instances where a local computer is being run on the UNIX operating system. Communication between these machines is principally over telephone lines by means of a specific UUCP protocol (UNIX-UNIX Copy), although there is now a move to make use of packet switching technology. The total user population is estimated to be about 30,000 comprising 50 mainly academic and research sites in the UK, 400 in Europe and a further 1,500 in the US.

In a number of instances it was reported that researchers were using the US ARPANET. Access to this facility is provided by University College, London which operates a relay service for UK academic traffic based on what is called the "Internet". The Internet has been referred to as a UK "network of networks" as it enables users to access other US academic networks such as MAILNET, BITNET and CSNET. The majority of traffic appears to comprise collaborative research projects associated with computing science, although there is also quite a heavy use of the mail relay service administered by UCL. Access to the Internet is available only to authorised users and is usually sponsored by research councils and other bodies, notably the Ministry of Defence. A protocol translation service is also provided by UCL to enable users to operate between different networking environments.

The library community, with few exceptions, had no option but to use PSTN dial-up connections, as in no single instance did they have direct access to campus networks. Consequently little use has been made of JANET and only limited use of PSS where access was available via a dial-up link to the computer centre. Access to PSS via the local network was eagerly awaited by library staff because of the cost benefits relative to PSTN.

Aside from the issue of users in areas other than those associated with computing having less convenient access to terminals, the number of networks available to users also depends on their being in a position to come to some arrangement regarding mechanisms for meeting the cost of networking outside the academic network (JANET). There is, in addition, a significant lack of information available to potential users in relation to exactly what type of network services are available, what they offer and how they can be used. In several instances it was remarked that many staff were unaware of JANET's own network services, particularly Grey Book mail. Computer centres conceded that a great deal remains to be done in educating and providing assistance to new users wishing to use networks for purposes other than data processing.

In general it appeared that computer users in the pure and applied sciences, representing the bulk of current network traffic, were well provided for in terms of user support and services. Libraries, by contrast, tended to operate independently of their computer centres and in consequence perhaps, were only able to provide limited network-based facilities to their clients. Their position was characterised as one of moving forward cautiously as they built up local expertise. Provision of adequate financial resources was also a major element in the rate at which terminal-based services could be contemplated, particularly in the context of mounting on-line public access catalogues and other information services which could be accessed via the campus network. Libraries that demonstrated significant progress in this direction were usually those which had forged a particularly close and harmonious working relationship with the local computing service based on a mutual understanding of their respective needs and priorities.

3.1 WHO USES NETWORKS?

As one might expect, the bulk of network traffic is generated by computer centres themselves and by the established computing community in the pure and applied sciences. Network access was observed to fall into the following categories:

(a) access to national computer centres;
(b) resource sharing between sites;
(c) software distribution;
(d) multi-site research collaboration;

(e) database access;
(f) human communication, i.e. electronic mail and conferencing.

The majority of network usage is associated with transferring relatively large quantities of data between computing facilities. File transfer traffic was reported by one national computer centre to be running at a rate of some 1,500 calls on a busy day.

High-speed network development relating to Cambridge rings and ethernets has also involved computer centres in the implementation of new operating software, particularly to enable network interfaces between these new technologies and existing X.25-based campus networks. Consequently it was not uncommon to find software being transferred via JANET between, for example, Edinburgh and Kent.

Resource sharing and multi-site collaboration continues to play a major role in the current complexion of the networking scene. This type of network application is most prominent in the extensive arrangements that exist between the Science and Engineering Research Council and its many grant-holders based at universities and polytechnics throughout the country. SERC-sponsored networking catagories are broken down as follows:

engineering;
computing;
nuclear physics;
science;
astronomy.

Sponsored access to networks such as the ARPANET appeared in the main to be provided by SERC, the Computer Board and the Ministry of Defence. A variety of other interests were identified, including:

Medical Research Council;
National Environment Research Council;
British Telecom;
Numerical Algorithms Group;
Imperial Cancer Research Group;
US Department of Defense.

The impression gained was that most network use was concerned with data processing applications rather than human communications. Although the Internet at UCL represents traffic as mail messages in their technical report (18), closer inspection showed that difficulties had been encountered with the file transfer mechanism and consequently files have been sent under a mail message "envelope".

Database access by individual users or departments was difficult to pinpoint as once access to PSS had been arranged with a local computer centre traffic was monitored for the purposes of passing on Telecom charges only and not by network account as these are sent direct from the database vendor to the registered user. Libraries, however, consistently reported the popularity of services such as LEXIS, EUROLEX and to a lesser extent LAWTEL. In some instances law faculties had made their own arrangements for departmental access. While most libraries had Prestel terminals they reported that usage was not high apart from demonstration purposes and many members of staff in the business studies area who used financial data to prepare case studies. Prestel was used on a casual basis for snippets of information. In one instance access charges had been reduced in an attempt to stimulate demand.

It has already been observed that many libraries still use PSTN to access databases and consequently can offer only a limited service to users because of the costs involved. In at least one case efforts were made to use mainly European database hosts, particularly when the dollar exchange rate was unfavourable.

Only a few libraries had attempted to use JANET to access information held by other academic libraries. Two reported having used the network to access the EDCKFY database of EEC publications held by Dundee University. It was recognised that networking between libraries might promote greater opportunities for co-operation in the future and facilities such as mail might prove useful for exchanging information concerning the introduction of new computer-based services. Of particular interest to two universities has been the possibility of establishing network connections with their local bookshops to enable the introduction of on-line reporting and account management software - leading eventually, it was hoped, to a system offering paperless transactions, invoicing etc. In this instance network connection had been via a PSTN dial-up link to the bookshop's computer.

A computer centre currently examining the prospects of mounting a campus-wide teletext facility also voiced interest in putting up a bookshop bulletin board relating to set books, new titles published by members of staff, special promotions etc., although it is unlikely that it will be possible to use JANET in any connection relating to commercial interests.

In most instances university administrative functions, though computer-based, operated as a separate networking entity. Problems associated with students "hacking" into confidential data and possible difficulties concerning the Data Protection Act were the most common reasons advanced for maintaining an independent computing facility. (It was noted that UCCA has applied to use JANET which, if approved, would lead to an exchange of confidential data on the academic network.)

There was also evidence to suggest that library co-operatives would like to have access to JANET, but an earlier application was turned down principally on the grounds that the commercial nature of their relationship with libraries put such a proposition beyond the licensing terms under which the academic network is constituted. It was felt that once a precedent had been set it would be difficult to deny access to other library services and interested parties including publishers.

There appeared little doubt that at the present time academic networking is dominated by data communications relating to computational processes. As networks were originally developed precisely for this purpose it is perhaps not surprising the subsequent developments have tended to follow this course. Significantly improved connectivity provided by JANET will almost certainly lead to a rise n network traffic and some concern has been voiced by the computing community that the introduction of more services and thereby greater numbers of new users, might de-stabilise the operation of the existing network. Consequently network management is going to be of critical importance in the future, particularly if students operating portable workstations wish to access campus networks. Services like on-line public access catalogues may only prove a practicable proposition beyond immediate library premises after the introduction of high-performance local networks, which will be better equipped to deal with the high volumes of network traffic that will inevitably result.

At the present time computer centres appear to be concentrating on implementing wide-area standards (the Rainbow Books) and up-grading campus networks in response to local demands, largely from the established computing community, whose needs tend to be articulated in terms of improved data communication facilities with an emphasis on speed, volume, flexibility and reliability. Human communication (which will be dealt with as a separate issue) remains fairly low down on the list of local networking priorities.

3.2 RATE OF GROWTH OF NETWORKING

It is not possible to give precise figures relating to the overall growth in the rate of networking, but discussions with the Joint Network Team and university computer centres indicated that it is expected to rise steadily as connectivity continues to improve. The actual number of academic networks has been reduced since the appearance of JANET and rationalisation has thus significantly simplified the networking medium and the conditions in which it can now be offered as a practicable service to a wider category of users.

> "The management of the SERCNet has passed to the Network Executive and SERCNet became part of JANET in April [1984]. This has resulted in increased connectivity between academic sites." (19)

Network traffic at the Internet, monitored by UCL, has also risen, as noted in their technical report for the period 1983-84: "The level of usage, and the number of approved users had continued to increase." (20)

All universities reported an expansion of local terminal populations connected to campus networks and it may not be unreasonable to suppose that as access becomes more convenient demand for network-based services will increase. Once the value of electronic mail and conferencing becomes more generally recognised it is possible, however, that network traffic may reach levels sufficient to degrade the quality of service for all users. Even at the Internet, whose usage must be accounted for in "real cost" terms, it has been necessary to consider imposing limits on particularly heavy users.

> "Traffic estimates of tunnel usage have indicated that control may need to be exercised on the use of this route by those whose communication costs are centrally funded. Consequently a resource allocation scheme has been devised whereby the grant is divided into chunks (of nominally £25)... as they are used up further ones are allocated whilst available." (21)

There was no such rise in networking reported by libraries. It was conceded that on-line access for public users is running at an artificially low level. No great effort was being made to promote these services, as current budgetary and manpower constraints are insufficient to meet any rise in demand. Charging policies for on-line searches varied between institutions: at one end of the spectrum no charge was made, at the other full charges were always levied. The average charge appeared to be in the region of about 25-30 per cent of actual costs.

Several libraries were looking at the possibilities of purchasing stand-alone systems, either direct from commercial suppliers such as GEAC or from a library co-operative. This would have the effect of replacing wide-area network access via PSTN for the purposes of on-line management systems like the circulation file, accessions, ordering etc. as these types of applications are now capable of being operated on in-house facilities. Further cost reductions will be possible by their eventual connection to campus networks enabling access to PSS for database searching and on-line cataloguing.

Networking between libraries on JANET may increase as staff become more familiar with the technology and at least one library co-operative expressed concern that machine-readable records might be occasionally exchanged in this manner instead of by licensed agreement.

In summary, the rate at which networking will grow was observed to relate in the main to economic issues concerning mechanisms for meeting the "real" costs associated with accessing on-line services, and those involved in using the public network - whether it be PSS or PSTN. The provision of convenient access to communications equipment, its ease of use, the availability of local expertise and sufficient numbers of trained library staff to support the expansion of network-based user services were identified as other key factors affecting the extent to which networking can be introduced in a wider context than appears possible at the present time. Limits to growth might also arise depending on the eventual volume of traffic generated as a result of improved connectivity, the implementation of new services and a corresponding rise in the numbers of registered computer users.

3.3 INTERACTIVE OR NON-INTERACTIVE NETWORKING?

The concept of interactive and non-interactive networking proved difficult to define in computing terms as it depends entirely on the nature of the task being performed. For this reason there was some variance in the responses from computer centres. In the context of networking with international hosts non-interactive working is encouraged as it reduces the need for "real time" terminal access. UCL operates a mail relay service for registered users to the Internet which means that it is not necessary for them to consult remote mailboxes independently. All mail is instead sent to UCL and forwarded to individual users with a consequent reduction in network traffic:

> "Clearly this facility has become a very important part of our service saving at least 50% of the potential mail traffic on the US to UCL part of the relay."(22)

File transfer, which is a non-interactive process, appeared to be one of the most popular services provided by JANET. Users prefer to prepare material on local systems whose editing facilities, for example, they will have become familiar with over time. Interactive network access often requires data to be manipulated in a "foreign" computing environment and therefore it was considered that the growth of interactive working over the wide area networks was not an automatic consequence of better connectivity.

Electronic mail and conferencing also operate on the basis of non-interactive working in the sense that one does not require to be in direct contact with a mail recipient or conference participant. Indeed this is one of the benefits of such a facility as it enables conference entries or messages to be entered at the convenience of users, with the assurance that they will reach their destination regardless of whether the recipient is personally contactable at any particular time. Entries are automatically stored on the mailserver and can be read and sorted off-line at leisure.

Where interactive network connections are essential it is usually in the use of on-line databases, particularly where information is updated on a regular basis, e.g. in the provision of "volatile" financial information. While dangerous to generalise, in the opinion of those associated with networking it would seem that interactive access is nearly always necessary for consulting information-based networks that enable users to "move about", to search, retrieve and where permissable download data. In the context of data processing, in the computing sense, the decision to adopt interactive or non-interactive modes of working will depend on the objectives of a particular operation and the range of network services available (in some instances only terminal access may be feasible). Human communication does not require interactive working, although interactive computer messaging systems do exist. In short, future trends will be task-related with improved interactive access emerging as an option where required.

3.4 MESSAGING

Facilities like electronic mail and computer conferencing had been given a low priority at all the institutions visited for this survey. Each operated fragmented local mail systems mounted on a variety of departmental machines, but these could in no sense be considered as a campus-wide service available to all categories of users. Departmental mail systems were used in the main by students, although in several instances staff had begun to use this means to display general information relating to work assignments, tutorials etc. For a practicable local mail service to emerge it was considered necessary to install dedicated mailservers covering each university site, capable of being accessed from any terminal on the campus network. This would, in addition, require a considerable amount of work to be done in providing local directory services to enable users to identify the mailserver on which a particular individual's mailbox was located. Resources for this type of operation in both financial and manpower terms will be substantial and it was felt that until there was sufficient demand it was unlikely that these would be diverted from the development of other local network services for which there was a clear demand among existing computer users.

Wide-area mail systems had been in use between computer centres for some time and were recognised as a useful and effective means of communication. However, the reasons for their adoption in this area also indicate why the service has not been taken up by many other categories potential of users. As stated earlier, most computing staff have access to personal terminals located in their own offices; are familiar with networking practices and have little difficulty in establishing colleagues' network addresses - thus the prospects of being able to contact people at other computer centres is relatively high for the same reasons.

By contrast, users outside this specialist area cannot rely on colleagues who do not have such convenient access to a terminal making regular checks on their mailboxes or indeed even having access to facilities like Grey Book mail (which remains to be implemented at a number of institutions). Many universities stated that they intend to participate in the Name Registration Scheme, but so far very few of those consulted had fully registered the network "names" of their local computing facilities. By analogy one could say that at the present time few potential mail users have their own telephone, knowledge of area dialling codes or access to local directories and many are in any case unfamiliar with the operating procedures necessary to make a call.

The lack of user awareness and failure to provide adequate education was consistently identified as being a barrier to network access. Until staff developed a greater degree of computer literacy it was unlikely that there would be a significant demand for electronic mail and conferencing. While this situation remains future network development will in all probability continue to focus on applications associated with computation and data transmission.

This is, of course, a circular argument as until a fully functional mail structure is available few new users will be attracted to the medium. It was even hinted that this might be the intention of those who wish to keep network traffic at a manageable level sufficient to cater for the needs of established users (who, it was noted, placed no urgency on mail and conferencing).

Grounds for some optimism concerned the introduction of campus information services including teletext, bulletin boards and particularly on-line public access catalogues. OPAC's were seen to constitute a good example of a type of network application to which all staff and students could relate. The ability to consult the circulation file from a remote site and reserve books on-line without having to leave one's office or department was considered to offer the best prospects for motivating the "computer naive" user. It had also been observed that those who currently used mail and conferencing systems had first been introduced to these services through the use of computers for other purposes which gives added weight to the importance attached to introducing campus-based information systems. This also reinforces the view that as networking evolves it will be necessary for much closer liaison to occur between computer centres and libraries. This point was alluded to by the Joint Network Team in relation to the future role of computer centres:

"Many believe that computer centres will be transformed into departments for Information Technology in which the key components will be the local networks..."(23)

Libraries as the foremost providers of information to the academic community will require to interact with computer centres as their services can play an integral part in extending computer literacy, which in turn may lead to a greater demand for network-based, computer-mediated human communication.

3.5 COSTS

The question of cost in relation to network access at universities proved to be an intractable issue, due in part to the nature of university funding and also to the changes that have occurred since the introduction of the Joint Academic Network. Facilities like electronic mail and conferencing are at such an early stage of development that it is possible only to advance an impressionistic view based on interviews with computer centres and the Joint Network Team.

Access to academic networks such as those in the US including ARPANET, MAILNET, CSNET etc is provided almost exclusively by sponsoring bodies, such as SERC, and cost comparisons for the use of different networks are not available. Internet rates for terminal calls to the US, quoted at 26p per Kbyte and 12p per minute, "will not stay constant as the efficiency of the underlying transport mechanism is improved".(24)

Changes in costs were commonly attributed to technical developments rather than any reduction in access charges levied by the networks themselves. Cheaper hardware, the development of more sophisticated software and faster data transfer rates were all contributing to a more effective use of the networking medium. Standardisation and rationalisation of network routes had also led, for example, to a dramatic reduction in PSS usage at universities and a phasing out of redundant leased-line connections now superseded through the extent of network connectivity provided by JANET.

The above arrangements relate essentially to the computing community whose networking arrangements have been co-ordinated at a national level. For those who wish to access commercial networks such as libraries and individual users the position is less straightforward. Computer centres operate a strict control over access to the PSS gateway and users in particular, are required to apply for an account number on the understanding that they are personally responsible for meeting all Telecom charges attributable to their use of, for example, Telecom Gold. They must, in addition, make their own arrangements with network vendors for meeting membership charges. Actual use of commercial networks by individuals was not reported to be great and most computer centres prepared manual accounts relating to PSS charges which indicates how low the level of access must be at the present time.

Since the Computer Board intends to withdraw its subsidy to computer centres for the use of PSS now that JANET has become established as the principal route for academic traffic, arrangements exist to provide local accounting packages linked to PSS gateways. A number of institutions have been operating this system and are confident that they will be capable of monitoring and billing PSS traffic by individual account number. As demand increases it will be necessary to automate the billing process itself, but, as indicated above, this has not yet been necessary.

The question of costing network access is one which has not been fully resolved in the academic community, particularly in relation to the future information needs of libraries and individuals whose requirements are for human communication facilities unassociated with computing per se. This area was described as "a black cloud of uncertainty" by one librarian and currently represents a serious impediment to the adoption of networking as a utilitarian commodity on a par with the telephone.

Recent studies in the US and Sweden have demonstrated that electronic mail and conferencing can be an extremely effective medium in relation to the costs of long distance telephone calls and face-to-face meetings. Of the 42,000 inter-institutional messages generated by some 6,000 individual US MAILNET users between 1 September and the end of 1984 over 80 per cent of MAILNET messages cost less than 50 cents and over 50 per cent under 20 cents. In Sweden it has been calculated that messaging on COM cost an average of £7 per hour or about 8p per read message. It was therefore cheaper than the telephone for short messages, cheaper than ordinary mail and cheaper than face-to-face meetings where the group size was larger than 15 - significantly cheaper if participants had to travel to a meeting.

Details of four major commercial on-line services including electronic mail and telex facilities are given in Appendix A from which it will be seen that costs vary considerably, particularly in relation to minimum monthly charges which range from £5 to £40. Mailbox rental also varies from nil to £30 per month, and in most cases special operating software is required which can cost between £75 and £199 (excluding VAT). Given, in addition, that one must know which systems are being operated by colleagues and the procedures necessary for obtaining local Network User Indentities (NUIs), arranging for billing and payment for network membership, Telecom charges etc, it is not difficult to deduce at least part of the reason for the relatively low take-up of these services among the academic community.

The experience of computer centres in operating electronic mail and the COM computer conferencing system hosted at York University have both demonstrated the potential of computer-mediated human communication using the academic network. Were these facilities to be developed, significant savings could be made in postal, telephone and travel expenses. Adequate resources and expertise do not appear to have been allocated to these areas on the evidence of this survey. The Joint Network Team hoped that the situation would change over the next two years as experience of what are relatively new networking practices is consolidated. The priority appears to be ensuring the reliability and stability of the network before implementing too many new services that might overwhelm the current management capacity of local computer centres.

3.6 COMMERCIAL INTERESTS

Academic publishers, library services, co-operatives, and the booktrade all demonstrated an interest in networks, although their degree of involvement varied considerably.

The publishing industry was concerned about the effect networks might have on its ability to secure an equitable revenue from the sale of information via on-line databases. Consequently, with the assistance of the Publishers Association, an agency called Publishers Databases Ltd was set up in 1982 to act as an intermediary between information providers and database vendors. Its brief has been to examine brokerage agreements and to assist small publishers in particular to negotiate contractual terms on the basis of an agreed common policy approach. This would prevent them from being "picked off at will" by large international database hosts who might otherwise play them off one against the other.

Academic publishers have taken a cautious approach to the question of networks. A recent survey (25) demonstrated that of 526 publishing houses spanning a wide range of interests only 1.2 per cent had accepted author-generated text by means of the telephone network and even fewer, 0.8 per cent had used this method to convey text to the printer. In the opinion of several academic publishers the use of networks as a means of capturing text cannot as yet be justified on economic grounds when compared with conventional methods of originating large amounts of text comprising technical setting and complex illustrative matter.

> "To date we have not used this route for the transmission of manuscripts, apart from a few test runs. Problems with speed, poor line quality and mathematics are significant factors in discouraging our use of electronic mail as a means of collecting material for publication... The clumsiness of communicating through the telephone network is undoubtedly a major factor in deterring us from using on-line services."

Some hesitation was evident among publishers regarding the best way to approach the use of computer-based delivery systems and whether to opt for marketing their products on-line or to adopt a 'stand-alone' medium such as compact or video disks.

> "At the moment a watching brief is being kept on all these developments and the emergence of networks is an example of one such application. As more people become familiar with the technology and have access to the hardware and an understanding of the software such systems will become more practicable."

In general more attention was being given to examining the marketing potential for computer-based product than to installing new technology systems concerned with in-house text processing: "The fear of disruption to schedules through change is a strong factor in keeping old methods going."

Library services and co-operatives were alert to the trend towards stand-alone management systems and were developing their own services in this direction. A number of university libraries already operate GEAC "turnkey" in-house computer installations and this survey indicates that several more are actively considering this possibility. Many were attracted by the advantages offered by greater local control of automated systems and software management packages that provide an integrated operation covering accessions, cataloguing and circulation. It was also felt that recurrent costs might be reduced by comparison with the present combination of computer-based management services, particularly those involving on-line transactions.

Systems like Perline and Bookline (for handling periodicals and book acquisitions) have now been amalgamated in a package called PEARL offeredby Blackwell Technical Services. A completely self-contained system, PEARL is marketed to libraries as providing independence and local automomy, "under your control and available whenever you need it".

At least one library co-operative's stand-alone package will offer electronic mail as an option, which will enable users operating similar systems to contact each other directly. This was considered to be particularly attractive for polytechnic libraries who are unable to access JANET and Grey Book mail. It was clear that in meeting a growing demand for stand-alone management systems competition between vendors is likely to be keen in securing existing custom as well as generating new markets.

The book trade has been using networks for some time, the best known of which is teleordering. The concept of a viable network population is illustrated by the mixed fortunes of this network. At the time of writing there were in the region of 30 participating publishers and some 200 order points throughout the country. This relatively low level of connectivity has been regarded as insufficient to make the network fully effective. What has been termed a "log jam" resulted as booksellers waited for more publishers to join the network and vice versa. A recent initiative called Project 84, financed largely by the publishing industry, attempted to improve network membership by providing terminals to bookshops on a trial basis. The network itself has made efforts to improve access by offering the service via a Prestel terminal, where before bookshops had to acquire dedicated hardware which for small businesses was a not insignificant item of expenditure. It remains to be seen whether access will attract more booksellers to adopt the teleordering and if more publishers reciprocate by participating themselves.

Regional and local computer networks are also used by the booktrade as a means of linking remote branches, enabling central ordering and improved stock control. Books can be moved between branches according to demand by means of on-line stock reporting - ordering can also be performed on-line and co-ordinated centrally by the main branch.

At a local level there is a trend towards the integration of all computerised operations from point-of-sale to invoicing, accounting and stock control. The introduction of bar coding will constitute the basis for systems such as these and large retail chains like WH Smith have been putting considerable pressure on publishers to co-operate by including bar codes on covers and book jackets. WH Smith has also taken the lead in promoting the adoption of an industry standard for electronic invoicing. This scheme, if adopted by the booktrade, may be based on the Article Numbering Association (ANA) TRADACOM standard called TRADANET, which provides a common 'envelope' and 'addressing' protocol capable of using "a common carrier [PSTN/PSS] for business transactions and general communications in the book-related communities".

The keynote for the booktrade appears to be one of flexibility. Dedicated hardware is now being superseded by equipment that is capable of being built upon and expanded as expertise increases. A large bookselling chain estimated that since the introduction of new technology it had increased stockturn by 9 per cent and reduced stockholdings by approximately 17 per cent - a saving of £140 000 (on an annual turnover of £3.5m).

The level of interest in computer-based systems for bookshops was reported by the Booksellers Association to be "gradual but steady", and requests for information - particularly from small bookshops - has led the BA to compile a step-by-step guide for members contemplating the purchase of computer equipment.

A striking similarity with libraries was observed in regard to future requirements. Both bookshops and libraries appear to be moving in the direction of integrated, self-contained management and information software packages based on one common operating system which can be accessed locally or remotely by other branches. Elements of these network-based facilities will eventually be offered on a public access basis to customers and library users.

University bookshops, particularly those cited on a campus, are in principle, ideally situated to provide on-line information services and book ordering management systems relating to library accessions. In practice, however, it appears that only those that are wholly owned by their parent institutions, such as Leicester and Warwick for example (i.e. not part of a commercial retail chain) may be in a position to explore the provision of these facilities, which require access to the university's private local network. By means of the teleordering network, Prestel and the university network certain bookshops may find themselves straddling two or more networking environments, assuming the role of an electronic clearing house for local orders and enquiries. In the event of bookshops in the category mentioned above also having access to JANET, it may be possible for them to serve institutions, other than their own - particularly in instances where there are several other universites in the immediate vicinity. Commercially-based concerns, however, be they library co-operatives, or branches of large retail booksellers are unlikely to gain access to academic networks such as JANET. Whether local university networks constitute a separate case remains to be established.

It has been observed that publishers in the UK have not yet adopted the public data network to any marked extent as a means of capturing keyed text. However, authors based at universities are now in a position to use the academic network to communiate with co-authors, series editors and advisors. The networking medium will also provide a source of on-line information, as several institutions have mounted local data sets including, for example, census data, data from the Meteorological Office, trade statistics etc. The preparation of references may also be a less painful process if authors are able to interrogate library workstations. Specifically subject-orientated on-line newsletters or bulletin boards will provide a valuable means of keeping authors in touch with recent developments in their disciplines, and can act as a forum for comments and queries. A recent example in this connection is the development of a network-based bulletin board for the humanities funded by the British Library, which will be launched in the autumn of 1985 by the Office for Humanities Communication based at the University of Leicester.

4 Summary of case studies

CASE STUDY 1

Institution: University - Large Civic

Computer Centre

LAN TECHNOLOGY: pilot X.25 CPSE (campus packet-switching exchange)
IMPLEMENTATION: October 1984
TERMINAL POPULATION: 500
JANET IMPLEMENTATION: October 1984
RAINBOW BOOKS: All services except job transfer (Red Book)
CAMPUS MAIL: No campus-wide facility
NETWORK ACCESS PRIOR TO JANET: GANNET (North-West Universities Network), SERCNet, PSS
NETWORK ACCESS SINCE JANET: PSS, JANET
NAME REGISTRATION SCHEME: Not fully registered
LOCAL MAIL DIRECTORY: No
PSS: Retains independent PSS gateway

Library

LAN CONNECTION: No
NETWORK ACCESS: PSTN dial-up
CO-OP MEMBERSHIP: No
MAIL: No
JANET USAGE: None
PRESTEL: Yes
OTHER NETWORK CONNECTIONS: Local university bookshop

In addition to providing local computing facilities this institution is funded by the Computer Board as a national computer centre and occupies a key position in the structure of the Joint Academic Network operating as a JANET packet-switching exchange (JPSE) and network operation centre (NOC). Prior to the introduction of JANET it was also the hub of a regional "star" network providing computing support to neighbouring institutions.

Given this background the high level of local expertise plays a major part in network development and it was planned to extend the terminal population distributed across the campus network to 1000 workstations over a period of twelve months.

Human communications services such as mail had not been expressed as a high priority by users. At the present time there is no campus-wide mail system but "piecemeal" provision exists on several departmental machines. It is hoped to rectify this position when finance is available by providing dedicated mailservers at each site which will be connected to the campus network. The bulk of current network traffic is generated by researchers working in the pure and applied sciences with up to 1500 file transfer transactions per day.

Priorities for the future were expressed in terms of implementing job transfer (Red Book) and improving the reliability of their existing services including the development of improved operator interfaces associated with datafile processing and job status reporting.

The library remains to be connected to the campus network. Dial-up PSTN connections were being used for access to databases and on-line cataloguing services. Plans exist for introducing an on-line public access catalogue the installation of which it is estimated will cost in the region of £600,000. The introduction of this service will take place in two stages phased over five years. In the immediate term it is planned to operate a terminal-based in-house library information service for users as a stop-gap measure from October 1986.

A network link has been established between the library and the university bookshop for the purposes of experimenting with the possibility of introducing paperless transactions and on-line order status reporting. To date trials have proved impressive, enabling orders to be recovered by a variety of search parameters including date, supplier, author, title and subject in almost any combination.

The university has retained its own independent PSS connection and the library hopes to benefit by using this service via the campus network as a means of reducing Telecom charges for PSTN connections to international database hosts. At the present time all charges for literature searches are passed on to the user.

The only instance of computer conferencing to be encountered was the chemical engineering department's use of COM hosted by the University of Stockholm.

CASE STUDY 2

Institution: University - Small Civic

Computer Centre

LAN TECHNOLOGY: X.25 CPSE
IMPLEMENTATION: April 1984
JANET IMPLEMENTATION: March 1985
TERMINAL POPULATION: 80
RAINBOW BOOKS: All services except job transfer (Red Book)
CAMPUS MAIL: Yes
NETWORK ACCESS PRIOR TO JANET: SWUCN (South-West Universities
Computer Network) SERCNet, PSS
NETWORK ACCESS SINCE JANET: JANET, PSS
NAME REGISTRATION SCHEME: No
LOCAL MAIL DIRECTORY: No
PSS: Retains independent PSS gateway

Library

LAN CONNECTION: No
NETWORK ACCESS: PSTN dial-up or via acoustic coupler to PSS gateway on university mainframe
CO-OP MEMBERSHIP: SWALCAP, since 1978
CO-OP SERVICES: On-line circulation (1978), cataloguing (1982)
MAIL: No
JANET USAGE: None
PRESTEL: Yes

The computer centre reported that since the installation of their JANET connection network access has been greatly simplified and full connectivity has led to a significant reduction in PSS traffic. Surprise was expressed by the rate at which departments were connecting to the campus network and it was planned to increase the distributed terminal population to 100 workstations over the next few months. Users were becoming increasingly reluctant to move between buildings to access computing facilities as it becomes possible to have more localised access via the campus network.

A mail system has been in operation for several years but its use appears to be restricted mainly to those already using terminals on a regular basis for computing purposes. The installation of a new PABX has provided an opportunity to wire up most offices as a pre-requisite for the provision of improved access to the campus network and it was hoped that as terminals become more generally available services such as mail will prove more popular. (It should be added that the PABX is not used to carry network traffic, common ducting is simply used to convey both telephone and campus network cabling.) Until the terminal population has been expanded and sufficient demand develops for a more extensive electronic mail system it was considered difficult to justify the work involved in mounting comprehensive directory facilities.

Grey Book mail is now available to users but its use once again tends to be concentrated among those within the computing community, particularly computer centre staff. It is not anticipated that the use of Grey Book mail will increase to any significant extent until people have more convenient access to desk-top terminals and through instruction and practise become more familiar with its operation.

The majority of network traffic involves transferring computing files to the major centres in London and Manchester and providing grant-holders access to SERC facilities which is now possible using JANET.

Access to PSS is strictly controlled and since its use must now be self-financing a full accounting package has been mounted on the independent gateway. It is anticipated that the majority of traffic on this facility will originate from the library and its requirement for IPSS connections to international database vendors in particular.

The library is not linked to the campus network and must therefore use a dial-up PSTN link, although it is possible to access the PSS gateway via an acoustic coupler which provides a connection to the computer centre.

Membership of a library co-operative involves a great deal of on-line working and the library is considering the purchase of a stand-alone management system such as that offered by GEAC. By mounting all their management files on an in-house facility it was hoped that some savings could be made, especially in the area of recurrent costs. (One institution consulted estimated that of its £78,000 annual co-operative membership costs £7,000 related to on-line transactions.)

The use of on-line literature searches had been kept at a conservative level and totalled 384 for the academic year 1983-84. At the present time searches are undertaken free of charge.

The library would like to introduce a terminal-based public access catalogue capable of expansion to include their entire collection. Operating both fiche and a computer-based system was not considered to be cost effective. (Yet another institution estimated that of the £67,000 required to mount a relatively modest on-line search/retrieval facility almost £40,000 could be saved annually on their existing budget for fiche.)

Doubts were expressed about putting the on-line catalogue on the campus network as it had been estimated that the number of ports on the library computer would be unable to handle the volume of traffic likely to be generated. There was, however, a role for a library information service or bulletin board offering non-catalogue information which could be accessed from the campus network.

At the present time two public access terminals are available in the library, both of which are connected to the library co-operative's mainframe computer. Using the circulation file this network connection has been used as an "ersatz" catalogue (a practice not recommended by library staff). Reservations can also be placed in this manner.

Future plans concerned with the provision of new network-based facilities will depend on the rate at which terminals are installed across the campus. Interest has also been expressed in interactive computer conferencing which may be considered as the network matures.

CASE STUDY 3

Institution: University - Campus Structure

Computer Centre

LAN TECHNOLOGY: X.25 CPSE and a series of Cambridge rings
IMPLEMENTATION: Cambridge ring (1980), X.25 (1981)
TERMINAL POPULATION: 350
JANET IMPLEMENTATION: 1 April 1984
RAINBOW BOOKS: All services
CAMPUS MAIL: Yes
NETWORK ACCESS PRIOR TO JANET: USENET, SERCNet, PSS
NETWORK ACCESS SINCE JANET: JANET, USENET, PSS
NAME REGISTRATION SCHEME: No
LOCAL MAIL DIRECTORY: Yes
PSS: Retains independent PSS gateway

Library

LAN CONNECTION: No
NETWORK ACCESS: PSTN dial-up or PSS connection via acoustic coupler link to computer centre
CO-OP MEMBERSHIP: No
MAIL: No
JANET USAGE: Yes, via computer centre
PRESTEL: No

In addition to providing local computing facilities this institution also acts as a UK relay for USENET whose European node is located in Amsterdam.
Academic and commercial traffic is redistributed to users throughout the country who use the UNIX operating system running UUCP (Unix-Unix CoPy). This network is not X.25 - compatible and therefore exists outside the JANET networking community.

In common with other institutions visited the number of terminals distributed over the campus network was being expanded and had risen from 320 at the end of 1984 to 350 by May 1985. A high-speed network is in operation running at an effective rate of 1Mb/s which it is planned to increase to 60Mb/s. This will make the introduction of a fully networked on-line public access catalogue a more practicable proposition as the X.25 network operates at only 9.6kb/s.

Although PSS traffic has been greatly reduced since the introduction of JANET the "slack" has been taken up by increased use of IPSS. (A typical Telecom monthly bill of £200 will generally be split between PSS/IPSS usage in the order of £198 to £2.) IPSS services are used by the library and also the university registry which exchanges messages with the University of Southern California with whom they operate a student exchange scheme.

Grey Book mail is heavily used by the computer centre as a means of receiving software from Edinburgh University's Regional Computing Centre - much of which relates to developing the local Cambridge ring.

The use of campus mail is largely between the computer centre and the science building, providing users with information about the status of computing jobs and general news about the availability of local services. Some members of research groups have access to the ARPANET via the Internet gateway operated by University College, London. Access to the Internet is via JANET or in cases where users are working from areas not yet connected to the campus network PSS can be used by prior arrangement.

The library is awaiting connection to the Cambridge ring and staff are currently investigating the provision of on-line services. As the library is not a member of a co-operative 10,000 machine-readable records based on the short-loan collection have been purchased from REMARC for evaluation. It was conceded that mounting a full OPAC was likely to take some time.

Wherever possible PSS was used to connect with databases hosts, of which DIALOG, BLAISE, DIALTEC, DATASTAR and EUROLEX had proved most popular. Access to these services is charged to the user, but at a subsidised rate (e.g. in the case of a literature search typically £10 per 100 citations plus 10p per additional citation).

JANET has been used via a dial-up link to the computer centre to access EDCKEY (European Document Centre Key - EEC official publications) held at Dundee University. This type of network application is not used to any large extent, but was recognised as a basis for future inter-library co-operation. The library was considered to be at an early stage in developing its use of networks and was "proceeding carefully as staff build up their expertise".

In the opinion of the computer centre, a great deal remains to be done in educating staff in the use of network services generally. It was hoped that the introduction of services such as an OPAC would serve to stimulate interest among those in the less computer literate areas of the university.

CASE STUDY 4

Institution: University - Collegiate Stucture

Computer Centre

LAN TECHNOLOGY: X.25-based network, Cambridge ring and GANDALF star-based network
LAN IMPLEMENTATION: X.25 (1983), Cambridge ring and GANDALF (1979-80)
TERMINAL POPULATION: 4-500
JANET IMPLEMENTATION: 1 April 1984
RAINBOW BOOKS: All services except job transfer (Red Book)
CAMPUS MAIL: No
NETWORK ACCESS PRIOR TO JANET: SERCNet, PSS, USENET
NETWORK ACCESS SINCE JANET: JANET, PSS, USENET
NAME REGISTRATION SCHEME: No
LOCAL MAIL DIRECTORY: No
PSS: At the JANET gateway

The complex structure of this institution makes networking between all its colleges and departments extremely difficult in practical terms alone. Colleges exist as autonomous bodies making co-ordination difficult, and there is no fully integrated institution-wide facility due to the variety of departmental computers in operation. Consequently services like mail were expressed as being no more than "a gleam in the eye" as they will require mail servers to be linked to every terminal on the network. As data lines leased from British Telecom are expensive and take time to install it was hoped to introduce a private system which could be wired at the same time as the PABX is due to be replaced.

Although some limited use is made of USENET (Unix) the main wide area network is now regarded to be JANET. A number of researchers also have access to ARPANET via the Internet at UCL. One of the main concerns to be identified with the principle of wide area networking related to cost and the question of "who would pick up the bill?". The overheads associated with controlling access, monitoring use and administering charges were felt to be the major factors likely to impede progress, particularly in the context of international networking.

The most popular network service was considered to be file transfer.
Introducing facilities like mail and conferencing will depend on the rate at which people become acquainted with using computers. The majority of mail users are already working with computers and in this context there was some evidence to show that once first-time users had mastered basic computing skills they were keen to extend their competence to include wider applications. More support was necessary for non-specialist computer users as there was still a great deal of ignorance evident concerning the potential of computer-mediated human communication.

This institution also faces particular difficulities where the automation of library services is concerned, as there are in the region of 180 libraries based in colleges, faculties, departments and special collections. The faculties of English, social sciences and modern languages have recently joined in an experiment to introduce computer-based library systems. It is hoped to provide ten terminals for each faculty library, seven of which will be on open access. This scheme is at an early stage of development and at the time of writing represented an intention rather than any existing operational system.

Both the British Library and OCLC are being considered as sources of machine-readable records and it is planned to have connections to either the X.25 or GANDALF local network which will in turn provide access to JANET and PSS. The specification for the minicomputer system on which this service will operate includes a provision for electronic mail (which will be used between libraries) and stand-alone library management software.

The introduction of an OPAC will mean that for the first time searches will be possible by means other than author name alone. It will, in addition, enable greater control of circulation and accessions, and a more comprehensive record of holdings will also be possible providing an opportunity for rationalising stock.

The hope was expressed that by installing an on-line public access catalogue accessible from the local network, users might be encouraged to use remote terminals. This was considered a likely trend if it were possible for academics and research students to check the loan status file and reserve books without having to leave their desks. The need was again stressed for more education to be provided for the less computer literate-particularly among staff.

CASE STUDY 5
Institution: University - Science/Technology Orientation

Computer Centre

LAN TECHNOLOGY: X.25 CPSE
IMPLEMENTATION: June 1984
TERMINAL POPULATION: 140
JANET IMPLEMENTATION: April 1984
RAINBOW BOOKS: Network service (Yellow Book)
CAMPUS MAIL: Yes
NETWORK ACCESS PRIOR TO JANET: GANNET, (North-West Universities Network), PSS
NETWORK ACCESS SINCE JANET: JANET, PSS
NAME REGISTRATION SCHEME: No
LOCAL MAIL DIRECTORY: No
PSS: Retains independent PSS gateway

Library
LAN CONNECTION: No
NETWORK ACCESS: PSTN dial-up
CO-OP MEMBERSHIP: BLCMP, since 1977
CO-OP SERVICES: on-line cataloguing, stand-alone circulation ("CIRCO")
MAIL: No
JANET USAGE: None
PRESTEL: Yes

The emphasis on network development at this institution concerned the need to improve data transmission rates and plans exist to install a high-speed ethernet next year, operating at 10Mb/s which will represent a significant advance on the present campus network which runs at 1200b/s. The university is spread over a number of dispersed buildings and fibre-optic and microwave links have been investigated as a means of providing high-performance physical connections. Ethernet technology has been adopted in preference to using a Cambridge ring-based local network because it was felt that since being adopted to such a large extent in the US it has become the industry standard, and thus offers better technical support and is likely to provide greater opportunities for further developments in the future.

The majority of network traffic reflects the requirements of the computing community for access to remote facilities based at Manchester and Queen Mary College, London. There are also members of staff who use the ARPANET via UCL as part of several research projects sponsored by SERC.

By comparison with other networking facilities there had been no significant demand for mail and at the time of writing Grey Book mail was not in operation, although it was hoped to implement the service during the summer. A local mail system has been operational for four years but was used mainly between students and the computing service. Local mail directory services were unlikely to be up-graded until the practicability of a national academic mail system is established. This will depend upon the rate at which institutions participate in the Name Registration Scheme. Once this occurs and demand for access to mail increases only then will the computer centre feel justified in allocating resources in this direction.

Since the introduction of JANET the level of PSS usage has dropped to such an extent that the computer centre currently meets all charges associated with access to the public network. Operating an accounting system for individual users is therefore unnecessary and at current levels of demand would not be cost-effective.

The library is not connected to the CPSE and plans to offer terminal-based services such as on OPAC will depend to a large extent on when connection can be made to the campus ethernet. In the short term it may be possible to introduce limited library information services on the CPSE network. Processing orders, invoices etc by means of network-based paperless transactions is also being investigated.

All network access is via a PSTN dial-up link and Telecom charges were described as a "black cloud" as the library is currently unable to use PSS. Network links (via PSTN) have been made to the University of York's on-line library facilities but only for demonstration purposes. Charges for literature searches have recently been reduced to about 20-25 per cent of the actual cost as usage had been running at such a low level. Prestel access was also low - the previous year's total usage amounted to only £146 in Telecom charges.

CASE STUDY 6
Institution: University - Humanities Orientation

Computer Centre
LAN TECHNOLOGY: X.25 CPSE
IMPLEMENTATION: 1980
TERMINAL POPULATION: 410 (approx.)
JANET IMPLEMENTATION: 1 April 1984
RAINBOW BOOKS: All services except mail (Grey Book)
CAMPUS MAIL: Yes
NETWORK ACCESS PRIOR TO JANET: SWUCN (South-West Universities Computer Network), SERCNet, PSS
NETWORK ACCESS SINCE JANET: JANET, PSS
NAME REGISTRATION SCHEME: Yes

LOCAL MAIL DIRECTORY: No
PSS: Retains independent PSS gateway

Library
LAN CONNECTION: No
NETWORK ACCESS: PSS via dial-up link to the computer centre
CO-OP MEMBERSHIP: SWALCAP, since 1976
CO-OP SERVICES: Circulation and cataloguing on-line
MAIL: No
JANET USAGE: Yes
PRESTEL: Yes

The computer centre hopes to replace the CPSE with a high-speed ethernet by October 1986, capable of operating ten times faster than existing Cambridge ring technology. A large proportion of network traffic is concerned with moving data between the local site, Manchester's Computer Centre and a CRAY computer based at the University of London Computer Centre. The CRAY link is used by meteorologists in particular. Although participants in the Name Registration Scheme, mail has not been assigned a high priority by network planners and Grey Book mail will not be implemented until January 1986. A local mail system has been in operation for about a year and is now heavily used by students, to the extent that provision for 60 000 mail messages has been allocated to serve in the region of 2,500 registered users. Staff have also begun to use his facility to leave messages for students and information concerning work assignments, deadlines etc.

Access to the network has been extended to halls of residence and two terminals are available at the main site on 24-hour open access. A number of students have applied to use the university's PSS gateway in order to use Telecom Gold. At the present time access is granted to students on the understanding that they will meet all PSS charges. A local accounting system is in operation which allows close checks to be made on personal traffic, but billing has to be dealt with manually.

A campus viewdata system is being considered, based on BBC microcomputers with colour monitors, and may include services such as news, career information, bulletin boards, job status reports from the computer centre and possibly an on-line public access catalogue with interactive facilities which will allow users to make book reservations on-line from local terminals.

The number of computer users in the humanities continues to grow. Introductory courses available to staff and students have been well subscribed and will be extended as part of a project development concerned with introducing computing for non-specialist users. A laser printer has recently been installed and is proving to be of particular interest to those working in the humanities. The multifont characteristics of the laser printer enable texts to be prepared using a variety of character sets, such as middle English, Greek, cyrillic etc. The ability to move simply from one font to another without having to change matrices has been received with considerable enthusiasm.

Although the library is not connected to the campus network it can access JANET and PSS via a dial-up link to the computer centre and has used this route to consult the EDCKEY database held at Dundee University, though not on a regular basis. Attempts are being made to reduce journal holdings by encouraging departments to make use of on-line database searches and the library offers SDI (selective dissemination of information) services to assist this process. Some departments have now made an allowance in their library budget allocation of about 5 per cent for "information services".

Library networking for the purposes of management services provided by membership of a library co-operative is performed on-line at the present time. A stand-alone system for circulation, accessions etc is being investigated and if approved will be based on software produced by the co-operative designed to run on a VAX 780 minicomputer. Plans to introduce locally networked services will depend on the rate at which the ethernet is installed. A limited on-line reservation service is available from two terminals in the library linked to the circulation file held by the library co-operative.

Networking is largely concerned with regular users based in the science community but the terminal population is being extended into the humanities area where the development of computer literacy skills has been given a high priority. Once local networking has been transferred to the ethernet it is hoped that all categories of users will be sufficiently familiar with operating skills to enable them to make immediate use of new services as they become available.

CASE STUDY 7
Institution: Polytechnic - Large Civic

Computer Centre
LAN TECHNOLOGY: Cambridge ring with X.25 gateway
IMPLEMENTATION: Some elements since 1983
TERMINAL POPULATION: 32 (Approx.)
JANET IMPLEMENTATION: February 1985 (SERC grant-holders only)
RAINBOW BOOKS: Network service (Yellow Book), terminal access (Green Book), file transfer (Blue Book)
CAMPUS MAIL: No
NETWORK ACCESS PRIOR TO JANET: SERCNet, PSS, ILEA polytechnic network
NETWORK ACCESS SINCE JANET: PSS, JANET (for SERC traffic only), ILEA network
NAME REGISTRATION SCHEME: No
LOCAL MAIL DIRECTORY: No
PSS: Only the computer centre may use JANET gateway for access to PSS

Library
LAN CONNECTION: Not fully integrated
NETWORK ACCESS: PSTN dial-up
CO-OP MEMBERSHIP: SWALCAP, since 1981
CO-OP SERVICES: circulation (1981), cataloguing (1984) on-line and stand-alone modes
MAIL: No
JANET USAGE: No
PRESTEL: Yes

Elements of a Cambridge ring local area network have been in operation for over two years and it was planned to extend the current terminal population to include each of the 15 sites that comprise this institution. The X.25 standard protocol for wide area networking has only recently been implemented on a VAX mainframe computer and difficulties had been encountered in obtaining the necessary hardware to provide a means of interfacing between the Cambridge ring and the X.25 gateway. It was again observed that US manufacturers are better placed to support ethernet technology as it has now become virtually an industry standard outside the UK.

Connection to JANET was provided in February 1985 but is only available to SERC grant-holders based at the polytechnic, which was a source of some frustration to computer centre staff.

There is no campus-wide mail system in operation, but machine-based mail is used by students who are regular users of departmental computers. Some staff have also begun to leave messages for students relating to work assignments. The administration area operates a separate mail system between deans and the Directorate. In general, however, a completely integrated mail facility is not likely for some time and will not be practicable until the Cambridge ring has been sufficiently extended.

The library is not as yet fully connected to the campus network and uses PSTN for all its wide area networking. As there are five libraries scattered over a number of sites plans exist to operate a stand-alone library management system based on a VAX 11/780 providing shared access to all libraries from a total of 80 terminals, some of which will be available for public access. Prestel is in use at three of the five libraries and a growing demand is becoming evident for the provision of more extensive on-line services, including access to databases such as LEXIS, EUROLEX and LAWTEL. At the present time each library can use their circulation file (based at SWALCAP in Bristol) as a limited form of on-line catalogue. It was felt that access to JANET would be a significant advantage for library staff for the purposes of inter-library co-operation.

CASE STUDY 8
Institution: Polytechnic - Small Civic

<u>Computer Centre</u>
LAN TECHNOLOGY: Cambridge ring with X.25 gateway

IMPLEMENTATION: October 1984
TERMINAL POPULATION: 30
JANET IMPLEMENTATION: April 1985 (SERC grant-holders only)
RAINBOW BOOKS: Network service (Yellow Book), terminal access (Green Book)
CAMPUS MAIL: No
NETWORK ACCESS PRIOR TO JANET: via dial-up PSTN only
NETWORK ACCESS SINCE JANET: PSTN and JANET (for SERC traffic only)
NAME REGISTRATION SCHEME: No
LOCAL MAIL DIRECTORY: No
PSS: No

Library
LAN CONNECTION: No
NETWORK ACCESS: PSTN dial-up
CO-OP MEMBERSHIP: BLCMP, since 1980
CO-OP SERVICES: circulation stand-alone, cataloguing on-line
MAIL: No
JANET USAGE: No
PRESTEL: Yes

Network access was described as being in a transitional phase of development. Work had begun on the installation of a Cambridge ring in October 1984, but at the present time terminals were grouped according to the location of mainframe computers although it was hoped to provide a greater distribution of access as the ring expanded. The rate at which local networking could be provided as a practicable service will depend on the level of resources available to the computing service. Several departments appeared to be placing greater emphasis on the provision of microcomputers of which there were already 400 spanning 40 different model ranges none of which was networked.

Electronic mail and conferencing systems were recognised as being important, particularly by research groups like those in education, industrial design and the Health Services Management Centre. Again the main barrier to offering such a facility was lack of financial resources. In this context the abilityfor all users to access JANET would be a distinct advantage if a national agreement could be reached regarding the position of polytechnics. Connection to JANET had been implemented in April 1985 but again only for SERC grant-holders. In general staff do not have access to PSS and any requirement for access to wide area networks is available only by means of PSTN dial-up links.

The library is not yet connected to the Cambridge ring but it is hoped to offer a limited OPAC service via a slow-speed dial-up access from departmental terminals from September 1985. This will offer loan status and searching by author, title and classification mark. The library would like to replace fiche altogether, which would represent an annual saving of £40,000, but the problem of introducing a terminal-based information service is in funding the initial capital installation costs estimated to be in the region of £27,000.

On-line searches have been kept at a fairly low level and 1983/84 expenditure was £5,500 by comparison to the overall library expenditure of £350,000. It was felt that access to JANET had certain attractions for the polytechnic library community in that it represents a network service that is effectively free to users. This position might not be extended to polytechnics were they to succeed in gaining access to the network and it is not yet clear exactly how costs will have to be met. So far as the relatively specialised requirements of the library community are concerned some doubts were expressed as to whether network routeing via JANET would prove to be simpler and faster in practice than exising PSTN connections due to the time sharing basis on which JANET operates. Direct network connection by means of a local PSS gateway might ultimately prove more effective.

[POSTSCRIPT: Since this survey was undertaken the author has been advised that the position of polytechnics regarding access to JANET may shortly be resolved. The view has been expressed at a senior level that there is now little doubt that it will be possible to arrange the licensing of JANET in such a way that the polytechnics can become full members of the JANET community, with full rights of connection. In addition, it may be possible for some other establishments, including, or example, the British Library to connect to JANET.]

5 Conclusions

Until relatively recently arrangements for access to networks from academic institutions required a considerable degree of computing expertise and were described by a leading computer centre as "arcane". The introduction of the Joint Academic Network clearly demonstrates a significant achievement in simplifying the procedures necessary for networking. The development of a set of standard protocols - the Rainbow Books - for use throughout the academic community is also acknowledged as a fundamental step in the process of ultimately securing an "open" networking environment based on international rather than proprietory standards.

This was the major national policy objective observed in the course of the survey. At the same time, developments aimed at greater standardisation and rationalisation, resulting in new opportunities, also raise significant policy and practical considerations identified below as requiring urgent attention if the full potential of the networking medium is to be realised - particularly in the context of services based on computer-mediated communication.

Before turning to the question of network access itself, it is interesting to note two findings of the Computer Board's report, published in 1983, relating to the provision of computing facilities for teaching: (5)

(a) "There is a critical lack of awareness in the academic community of the potential of the new technology and the likely changes it will bring to higher education. There is insufficient staff development in this area. At present no organised programmes of development exist to change the situation."

(b) "The implementation of hardware, software and communications on the scale required will require considerably greater numbers of computing support staff than exist in the universities at present."

Though stated originally in the context of providing adequate computing facilities for teaching purposes, these two factors alone remain perhaps the single most important issue upon which the future prospects of networking will depend if its application is to be extended to areas other than those concerned with computation and data processing.

1. Significantly more work requires to be done to improve current levels of computer literacy among academic staff. It was observed that in most instances those who had made efforts to explore network services such as electronic mail had done so as a consequence of being previously introduced to computers for quite unrelated purposes. Thus the development of even basic keyboard skills is a pre-requisite to fostering demand for the widespread adoption of such facilities on both an intra- and inter-institutional basis. Computer centres were unanimous in their reaction to the provision of services based on human communications: only when demand reaches sufficient levels will they be justified in allocating resources to developing local support in terms of better hardware (dedicated mailservers), software (including local directory services) and advisory back-up. At the present time those not fully acquainted with the networking skills often become frustrated and disillusioned with the medium due to their lack of expertise, poor or opaque documentation and a lack of facilities for tuition and support, resulting in wasted time and effort.

2. A national policy decision concerning computer-mediated communication is necessary. The need to co-ordinate and publicise these issues among the many interested, but disparate, groups that exist across subject disciplines is apparent. It has already been noted that facilities such as electronic mail can only be effective if there first exists a viable community of users. This in turn

depends on the extent to which individual institutions are prepared to introduce mail and other communications-related services as an integral part of local campus network developments. The national Name Registration Scheme represents an important move in this direction and it is to be hoped that more universities will support this initiative by registering and up-dating their local computer installations - at the same time mounting and maintaining site directories of registered computer users and their network addresses. Until this is achieved the complex procedures necessary for human communication to occur via computer networks will deter all but the most determined enthusiasts.

3. New and up-graded network services are evolving as a result of improved connectivity, and consequently larger distributed terminal populations. It will be necessary to monitor the manner in which these are adopted and the extent to which they meet the requirements of new categories of users whose needs may differ from those for whom the network was originally designed. In the course of the survey it proved extremely difficult to obtain an impression of how network traffic was divided between services such as, for example, electronic mail and file transfers. Statistics of this type do not appear to be readily available - if at all. In the context of network traffic overall, mail represents a very small proportion of current total loading. Possibly for this reason the extent to which different network services are used and for what purposes is not detailed separately. Experience gained early in the development of the ARPANET relating to the rapid rise in popularity of human communication over the network showed that planners were taken by surprise. At one university visited during the course of this survey where network monitoring had taken place, the computer centre had also been surprised at the extent to which the popularity of campus mail was evident among students. None of the libraries visited had access to electronic mail as such, but some were able to use on-line cataloguing record formats to pass electronic messages. Similarly, a number reported the use of circulation files as a means of accessing a crude form of on-line cataloguing facility. In both instances it was readily

admitted that these applications were less than satisfactory and not encouraged. It does, however, lend weight to the point that monitoring network services can highlight areas of difficulty and provide indicators to areas for future development. The inefficient use of networks enforced due to lack of adequate facilities also tends to result in users forming a poor impression of the medium.

4. The lack of adequate terminal provision is a major barrier to network access. Earlier research demonstrated that where people have to move physically between buildings, or even between floors in the same building, network services tend to be used less frequently than when a terminal is located in someone's own office. This renders electronic mail ineffective in particular, as to function efficiently "mailboxes" have to be regularly consulted. A number of universities are in the process of wiring offices for connection to the campus network, but outside of the computer centre itself few members of staff have access to a personal terminal. If the objective, stated by the Computer Board, is to provide at least one terminal per five students, then it is to be hoped that at least the same level of provision will be extended to staff. The provision of personal work-stations will enable networks to be used as a basis for inter-personal communication in a manner similar to that afforded by the telephone. For this to represent a practicable proposition more work will be necessary in simplifying existing procedures before the non-specialist will be persuaded to adopt networking between colleagues as a matter of routine. More accessible, user friendly interfaces and menu-driven software requires to be developed, capable of being used by less computer-literate members of staff and students alike.

5. Economic factors associated with networking constitute a major area calling for closer investigation. In the course of the survey it was widely acknowledged that, for example, methods of dealing with costing access to net-works outside JANET, and therefore representing "real" costs have not been fully evolved from the point of view of the individual user who may not be subsidised by a research council, or whose research project does not come

within the terms of any recognised funding category. In almost every instance network access involving PSS had to be sanctioned and paid for in full on a "pay as you use" basis, involving the issuing of personal account numbers and the operation of manual billing systems. Libraries constituted a separate case and had, in the main, to restrict the availability of network services to their clients because of budgetary constraints, relating not only to the direct costs of these services, but also to implications for the provision of adequate numbers of trained staff. In many instances only PSTN rather than PSS routeing for database access was possible, adding significantly to the cost of this type of network facility and resulting in its limited application. It is unlikely that this situation will improve until libraries are included in the extension of campus networks, thus providing more cost-effective means of network access. The inclusion of the library on the local network together with information-based services such as on-line catalogues and bulletin boards were regarded as the key to encouraging non-specialist users to develop keyboard skills, as they could all relate to utilities such as these. The need for more sophisticated computing facilities is becoming evident where libraries are concerned, and it is to be hoped that the UGC will recognise the importance of network-related information systems by making available a separate funding provision to be invested in planning and installing the technology-based facilities that will be necessary if high standards of service are to be maintained.

With the exception of the Internet administered by UCL and the Usenet relay operated by the University of Kent, access to other international academic networks appears to occur as a result of independent initiatives. Comparative costings and routeing strategies proved difficult to establish, which indicates that some mechanism for collecting and disseminating such information would prove a valuable service, as at a local level there appeared a considerable lack of awareness of what other institutions and research groups had achieved. (It is perhaps relevant to mention here that in at least one area - the humanities - a pilot on-line bulletin board available on JANET will shortly be offered by the Office for Humanities Communication at Leicester to fulfil just such a role.)

6. As campus networks become more sophisticated a greater degree of co-operation between libraries and computer centres will be necessary. Locally mounted network-based information services will require a pooling of expertise. In this connection there is an additional need to examine the practicability of co-ordinating related groups of network users whose activities may be even more closely aligned in the future. Areas like the computer centre and the library are obvious candidates: a number of institutions also mentioned recent experiments involving network links to bookshops. In one instance, noted in the survey, a campus-wide teletext system linking these three components was under discussion and had generated considerable interest. By combining these elements it may be possible to offer network services extending far beyond those which are possible by existing means of recording and transmitting information. A desire to integrate computerised information management systems was a recurrent theme evident among libraries, commercial library services and the book trade.

7. Finally there remains the question of network management. There is a need for a re-assessment of the issues affecting network access. Priorities need to be re-evaluated against a set of criteria which reflects the emergence of new categories of potential users who may wish to take advantage of the extent of network connectivity now available via JANET. The introduction of new services may depend on the rate at which the network can accommodate demands for up-grading and enhancing existing services based largely on data communications. It has also been argued that cutbacks in tertiary education have exacerbated a situation in which rapid change is unlikely to occur as the workload is spread among fewer skilled staff. Without provision of adequate financial resources it appears that network development is likely to be demand driven. The over-riding imperative of maintaining a stable network service, while eminently sound within the framework of current economic exigencies, may nonetheless result in

a more protracted phase of development for those services designed to embrace a wider constituency of users whose networking interests lie in areas unassociated with data processing.

Appendix A

Table B1 Cost-Comparison guide to four major on-line services (27)

	COMET	EASYLINK	ONE-TO-ONE	TELECOM GOLD
Means of access	Direct dial-up (local)	Direct dial-up (London - but regional shortly)	Direct dial-up (local)/PSS	Direct dial-up (local)/PSS
Services offered	Electronic mail, tele-messages, telex (send/receive)	Electronic mail, telex (send/receive), dial-a-gram, translations (French, Spanish, German).	Electronic mail, telex (send/receive), letters, courier (Greater London only at present), radio paging.	Electronic mail, express mail, telex (send/receive), telemessages, databases, noticeboard, radio paging, electronic publishing, diary facility
Registration fee	nil	£30	£50	£100 (with unlimited usage first month)
Mailbox rental	£30/month + £10/month for telex facility	£12/month	nil	nil
Connect time charges	nil	5p/min	30 secs free then 10p/min	10.5p/min
Telex to: UK	8p/200 characters	12.5p/200 characters	10p/200 characters	5.5p/100 characters
Europe	19p/200 characters	22.5p/200 characters	20p/200 characters	11p/100 characters
USA	61p/400 characters	65p/400 characters	35p/200 characters	16.5p/100 characters
Rest of World	102p/400 characters	110p/400 characters	65p/200 characters	115p/400 characters
Incoming telex	nil	nil (auto delivery 15p each)	nil	75p each
Electronic mail	nil	100 free, then 15p each	16p/1,000 characters	no charge
Storage charge	nil	nil	Short codes/distribution lists 10p per name	Filing charge 20p/unit (2,048 characters)
Software package	No charge for suitable software	£125 + VAT	£75 + VAT	£199 + VAT
Minimum invoice	£40/month	£36/month	£5/month	£10/month

Appendix B

Interview Questions for Computer Centres

1. Does your institution operate a local area network (LAN)?

2. What type of LAN technology is employed?

3. How long has the LAN been in operation?

4. When was the X.25 protocol first introduced?

5. Which computers are connected to the LAN?

6. What operating system is used?

7. What services does the LAN support?

8. What is the total terminal population on the LAN?

9. When was your JANET connection first implemented?

10. How many of the coloured book protocols are currently supported (e.g. job transfer, file transfer, terminal access, mail)?

11. What priority has been placed on mail and conferencing systems?

12. Is there a campus mail system, and if so for how long has it been operational?

13. What type of mail system is operated?

14. Is it possible to offer an impression of who uses the campus mail system, to what extent and for what purposes?

15. Based upon the experience of a campus mail system is it possible to hazard who will be most likely to use Grey Book Mail, to what extent and for what purposes?

16. If no campus mail system exists are there plans to install one?

17. Was your institution a member of a network prior to JANET?

18. Does your institution use any other networks since the implementation of JANET? If so, which and for what purposes?

19. What arrangements exist for network access on site?

20. Is it possible to indicate which wide area network services are most commonly used, by whom and for what purposes?

21. How are users authorised to access "real cost" services (e.g. PSS, IPSS, ARPANET, MAILNET, Prestel, Telecom Gold etc)? What accounting arrangements exit?

22. Do you use or intend to use the JANET Name Registration Scheme (NRS)?

23. Do you regularly update information from your site? If so with what frequency?

24. Do you maintain or plan to maintain a local support package?

25. What plans exist for introducing the new international standards planned to replace the rainbow books?

26. What problems can you identify associated with access to networks and their use for messaging, conferencing etc?

27. How, in broad terms, will JANET affect the economics of university computing?

28. Is the use of computer networks becoming more interactive rather than unidirectional?

29. Are there any trends in the current use of computer networks that may have implications for future network developments and network hosts?

30. Are there any identifiable trends relating to the rate of introduction of wide area networking?

31. Is there any evidence to suggest that services such as mail, conferencing and the joint writing of papers at a distance etc., will encourage greater use of computing facilities in the humanities area?

Appendix C

Interview Questions for Libraries

1. Is the library a member of a co-operative, if so which and since what date?

2. Which services offered by the co-operative are used by the library?

3. Are these services used in an on-line or stand-alone mode?

4. What minicomputer and operating system does the library use?

5. Does the system support electronic mail?

6. Is the library connected to a campus local area network?

7. What library services are available to users via the LAN?

8. What network-based library services are planned for the future (e.g. OPACs, bulletin boards etc)?

9. Does the library use dial-up facilities for on-line searching, or is connection now made via JANET? What advantages does the latter offer?

10. Does the library make use of the LAN's JANET connection for other purposes, if so for what purposes?

11. Can access be obtained to other library's computer-based records via JANET? Does this happen in practice, and if so for what purposes?

12. To what extent have computer networks affected the day-to-day running of the library?

13. What trends can be identified as a result of the growth and scope of computer networks?

14. What are the principal implications of computer networks for libraries in terms of user needs, technology options and operational costs?

15. What roles do public information services such as Prestel fulfil in the library?

Acknowledgements

The author wishes to thank the following organisations and individuals whose assistance was sought in conjunction with the preparation of this material.

The Booksellers Association
The Publishers Association
Mandarin Communications Limited
Blackwell Scientific Publications
John Wiley & Sons Ltd
Oxford University Press
Logica
Blackwells
Joint Network Team (JANET)
The Alvey Directorate
University of Stockholm Computer Centre (COM)
BLEND (Birmingham and Loughborough Electronic Network Development)
FERN (Further Education Research Network)
British Telecom
Brenda Moon, librarian, University of Edinburgh
Michael Emly, library technical services, University of Leeds
Mike Buckingham, Clinical Notes On-line, Elsevier-IRCS
Bill Tuck, University College London
Elizabeth Kilcoyne, EDUCOM (USA)
M. Wells, Director of Academic Networking (JANET)
Prestel
Micronet 800
Department of Industry
University of Leicester bookshop
Office for Humanities Communication, University of Leicester
British Library Research and Development Department

References

1. McCREDIE, John W. Campus information processing: a new wave. Educational Record, Fall 1981, p.6.

2. KAHN, Robert E. Proc. IEEE, 66 (11), 1978, p. 1304.

3. WELLS, M. The JANET Project. University Computing, Spring 1984, p.56.

4. COMPUTER WEEKLY. South-West X25 pioneers had vision, 10 November 1983.

5. COMPUTER BOARD. Report of a Working Party on Computer Facilities for Teaching in Universities, December 1983, p.11.

6. Interview with JNT, 19 February 1985.

7. EDUCOM Annual Report 1983/84, p.13.

8. McCREDIE, John W. and William P. TIMLAKE. Evolving computer networks in American higher education, EDUCOM Bulletin, Summer 1983, p.6.

9. HILTZ, Starr Roxanne and Murray TUROFF. The Network Nation, Addison-Wesley, 1978, p.21.

10. TELELINK. Prestel in figures, 1 (3), March/April 1985, p.4.

11. COM (Stockholm University Computer Centre). Experience with the Use of COM Computer Conferencing System, 1984, p.15.

12. EDUCOM Annual Report, p.16.

13. COM, p.31.

14. HILTZ and TUROFF, p.122.

15. UNIVERSITY OF DURHAM. Computer Centre Annual Report 1983-84, p.20.

16. KATZEN, M. Technology and Communication in the Humanities. Library Information Report No.32, British Library, 1985.

17. UNIVERSITY OF STRATHCLYDE. News Release, 24 January 1985.

18. KIRSTEIN, Peter T. and Tom DANIEL. UK - US Collaborative Computing Progress Report October 1984 - October 1985. Technical Report 103, University College London, October 1985, p.7.

19. KIRSTEIN, p.4.

20. KIRSTEIN, p.1.

21. KIRSTEIN. p.13.

22. KIRSTEIN, P 18.

23. COMPUTER BOARD. Joint Network Team Report for the Period September 1981 - December 1982. Rutherford Appleton Laboratory, Section 10.2.

24. KIRSTEIN, p.13.

25. MILLER, R. et al. Use of Word Processors by UK Publishers. Primary Communications Research Centre, 1984.

26. COM, p.38.

27. TELELINK, 1 (2), January/February 1985, p.47.

Select bibliography

ALTY, James. Computers for every student in Strathclyde University plan. Strathclyde University News Release. 14 January 1985, pp.4.

ANON. Easy access from a desk-top terminal. Times Higher Education Supplement. 23 March 1984, pp.28-29.

ANON. UK publishers press on with database venture. Communications Technology Impact. 4 (10), January 1983, p.2.

BINNS, S.E. Local area network developments in the UK. Data Processing. 25 (4), May 1984, pp.23-25.

BROWN, George et al. EDUNET: Report of the Summer Study on Information Networks. John Wiley & Sons, Inc., New York. 1967, pp.440.

BUCKINGHAM, M.C.S. Electronic mail. International Journal of Micrographics and Video Technology. 3 (2), 1984, pp.99-105.

C.E.C. APOLLO: Document Delivery by Satellite. Commission of the European Communities. Undated (received April 1985), pp.4.

CHARLES, Barrie J. Networking in the UK academic community. Proceedings of the Digital Equipment Computer Society, Coventry, UK. September 1982, pp.193-196.

COLE, Robert et al. Network interconnection at UCL. Department of Computer Science, University College, London. September 1984, pp.7.

COLE, Robert. User experience and evaluation of international X.25 services. Telecoms Today: Proceedings of the 1984 International Conference, pp.12.

COLLIER, Mel and PIPER, David. Multi-site library networking: experience of The Polytechnic of Central London. Program. 18 (2), April 1984, pp. 147-156

COMPUTER BOARD. Computer Board Policy. IUCC Bulletin. 5, Summer 1983, pp. 98-101.

COMPUTER BOARD. Joint Network Team Report for the Period September 1981 - December 1982. Rutherford Appleton Laboratory. 1983, pp. 56.

COMPUTER BOARD. Report of a Working Party on Computer Facilities for Teaching in Universities. December 1983, pp. 48.

COMPUTER BOARD. Topology of Joint Academic Network (JANET). Network Executive. April 1985, pp. 7 (unpublished).

CRAIGIE, J.A.I. Grey Book Mail in the UK. In EUTECO - European Teleinformatics Conference. K. Kalin, editor. Elsevier Science Publications (North-Holland). 1983, pp. 681-689.

DAVIES, H.E. Open Systems Interconnection: its value in university computing. February 1984, pp. 17 (draft paper).

D.O.I. Local area networks: report to the Focus Committee. Department of Industry. 1982, pp. 84.

EDUCOM. Annual Report 1983-84. Princeton, New Jersey, pp. 32.

EDUCOM. Mailnet: implementation to operation. EDUCOM Bulletin. Summer 1984, pp. 32-35.

FERN (Further Education Research Network). Invitation conference papers. 9 June 1984, pp. 60 (unpublished).

HILTZ, Starr Roxanne and TUROFF, Murray. The Network Nation. Addison-Wesley, London. 1978, pp. 528.

H.M.TREASURY. Information technology in the Civil Service. IT Series No. 9. HMSO 1985, pp. 82.

KATZEN, M. Technology and Communication in the Humanities. Library Information Research Report No.32. British Library, 1985.

KENNET, Donald. Varsities told to bring their networks into line. Computer Weekly. 29 May, 1983, p. 21.

KILLIE, Steve. Integration of electronic mail and conferencing systems. In Computer-Based Message Systems. H.T. Smith, editor. Elsevier Science Publications (North-Holland). 1984, pp. 261-269.

KIRSTEIN, Peter and DANIEL, Tom. The provision of UK - US services for non-subsidised users. University College, London (UCL Gateway Service Project). December 1984, pp. 10.

KIRSTEIN, Peter T. and DANIEL, Tom. UK - US collaborative computing progress report, October 1983 - October 1984. Technical Report 103. University College, London. October 1984, pp. 60.

LAMB, John. How computers can talk to each other. New Scientist. 9 September 1982, pp. 705-707.

LANCE, G.N. and POWELL, C.J. Early experience of using PSS at Avon Universities Computer Centre. IUCC Bulletin. 5, Winter 1983, pp. 147-152.

LOGICA. Alvey network study: network specification and implementation plan. Logica UK Limited. April 1983, pp. 62 (unpublished).

LOGICA. A survey of network-based services. Logica UK Limited. April 1985, pp. 65 (draft, unpublished).

McCREDIE, John W. and TIMLAKE, William P.. Evolving computer networks in higher education. EDUCOM Bulletin. Summer 1983, pp. 5-15.

McCREDIE, John W. Campus information processing: a new wave. Educational Record. Fall 1981, pp.6-11.

McCREDIE, John W. Gateways among academic computer networks. Cause/Effect. September 1984, pp. 32-33.

MANNING, G. Computing facilities provided by the SERC. Physics Bulletin. 34, 1983, pp. 236-239.

MARULAMA, Lenore S. Networking trends: reflections on their effect on technical services. Technical Services Quarterly. 1 (1) Fall 1983, pp. 221-231.

OAKLEY, B.W. Alvey and academics. University Computing. 6, 1984, pp. 10-15.

PALME, Jacob. Experience with the use of the COM computer conferencing system. Stockholm University Computer Centre. August 1984, pp. 67.

PULLINGER, David J. and Kate HOWLEY. The development of the Reference, Abstract and Annotations Journal (RAAJ) on the BLEND system. Journal of Librarianship. 16 (1) January 1984, pp. 19-33.

PURTON, Peter. Network profusion awaits standardisation. Infomatics. March 1984, pp. 74-75.

RICE, Ronald E. and CASE, Donald. Electronic message systems in the university: a description of use and utility. Journal of Communication. Winter 1983, pp. 131-152.

ROSNER, R.A. The transition towards open working. University of London Computer Centre. Spring 1984, pp. 10.

TUROFF, Murray and HILTZ, Starr Roxanne. Exploring the future of human communication via computer. Computer Compacts (Netherlands). 1 (2) April 1983, pp. 78-83.

VICKERY, Brian et al. Interactive information networks and UK libraries. Journal of Documentation. 40 (1), March 1984, pp. 36-49.

WELLS, M. The JANET project. University Computing. 6, Spring 1984, pp. 56-62.

WIGGINS, R.E. Distributed information processing: trends and implications. Aslib Proceedings. 37 (2) February 1983, pp. 73-90.

WILSON, P.A. Commercial Electronic Mailbox Systems. NCC Publications, Manchester. 1983, pp. 52.

WILSON, P.A. Introducing the Electronic Mailbox. NCC Publications, Manchester. 1983, pp. 196.

WINFIELD, Bob. Document transfer by satellite. Aslib Proceedings. 36 (4) 1984, p.9.